Still a Kid at Heart

My Life in Baseball and Beyond

Gary Carter and Phil Pepe

TRIUMPH
BOOKS

Triumph Books and colophon are registered trademarks of Random House, Inc.

Library of Congress Cataloging-in-Publication Data
Carter, Gary, 1954-
    Still a kid at heart : my life in baseball and beyond / Gary Carter and Phil Pepe.
        p. cm.
    ISBN-13: 978-1-60078-054-7
    ISBN-10: 1-60078-054-7
        1. Carter, Gary, 1954- 2. Baseball players—United States—Biography. I. Pepe, Phil. II. Title.
    GV865.C319A3 2008
    796.357092--dc22
    [B]

                                                    2007051714

This book is available in quantity at special discounts for your group or organization. For further information, contact:

Triumph Books
542 South Dearborn Street
Suite 750
Chicago, Illinois 60605
(312) 939-3330
Fax (312) 663-3557

Printed in U.S.A.
ISBN: 978-1-60078-054-7
Design by Sue Knopf. Production by Amy Carter.
All photos courtesy of Gary Carter unless otherwise noted.

THIS BOOK IS LOVINGLY DEDICATED TO MY WIFE, SANDY, for her unconditional love and devotion through our 33 years of marriage. Her dedication and support have been more than any man could ask for. She has been the best mom our children could want. Christy, Kimmy, and D.J. have turned out to be wonderful young adults, mainly because of her. She has been the backbone and strength to our marriage and the glue that has kept the family together. I am forever grateful and I will always love you.

Contents

Foreword

GROWING OLD IS MANDATORY; GROWING UP IS OPTIONAL, I've heard! As you read this story of Kid's life, you can decide to grow up like Gary, one of my favorite friends in baseball and in life. His passion and enthusiasm for baseball and life were infectious and even today his boyish charm reminds us all what it is like to be a kid again!

The grace with which he has dealt with setbacks, like the loss of his mom and dad, and the disappointments after retirement of being unable to participate in the game he loves, is truly commendable and an inspiration to us all.

Throughout it all, Sandy, the love of his life, has been at his side to support, encourage, and nurture him. A gifted athlete, an honorable man, and a good friend, but above all, Gary is a family man. His love for his family is abundantly apparent and brings him much happiness.

Gary was a hell of a catcher! He called a great game and commanded his position. His clutch hitting made him a Hall of Famer. What took so long for him to be elected, I don't know, but he has now taken his rightful place with the greatest catchers ever.

I hope Kid finds happiness in baseball again. He deserves it, and so does the game.

—*Johnny Bench*

Acknowledgments

I AM INDEBTED TO SO MANY PEOPLE WHO HAVE HELPED me throughout my life and career and in the preparation of this book.

My thanks to:

Ray Dumont of the U.S. Tour Golf.

Mead Chasky and Michael Katz for making sure all the *i*s were dotted and the *t*s crossed.

Phil Springstead, Tom Bast, and all the good, helpful folks at Triumph Books.

George Napolitano for his wonderful photographs. Andrea Graves for all the great family photos.

All my teammates and members of the four organizations with which I was affiliated: the Montreal Expos, New York Mets, San Francisco Giants, and Los Angeles Dodgers.

All my friends, too numerous to mention; if I did, I would have to write another book. To my children for their constant love and support.

And most of all, Jesus Christ.

1

In the Beginning

IT WAS SO QUIET, YOU COULD HEAR A CHAMPIONSHIP flag drop.

I was finishing up my second season as a member of the New York Mets, and after two years, I had no doubt that Shea Stadium, the home of the Mets in Flushing, Queens, was the noisiest ballpark in baseball.

From the jets flying overhead on those occasions when Shea was in the pattern of airplanes taking off and landing at nearby LaGuardia Airport, to the constant, incessant roar of the crowd on days and nights when Shea Stadium was filled to capacity, there were many times when the noise was so loud you could hardly hear yourself think.

This night, Saturday, October 25, Game 6 of the 1986 World Series, had been no different. From the first pitch, the crowd had been yelling, screaming, cheering, exhorting, a steady drone raining down from the stands as we battled tooth and nail with the Boston Red Sox—down 2–0 in the second, tied at 2–2 in the fifth, down 3–2 in the seventh, tied again at 3–3 in the eighth.

But now, as I walked to home plate with two outs and nobody on base in the bottom of the tenth, it was eerie. The silence was deafening. You couldn't believe 55,078 people could be so quiet.

The Red Sox had scored two runs in the top of the inning and the crowd sensed the inevitable. Everything we had accomplished over the past seven months—108 wins, the most in the Mets' 25-year history; being 21½ games ahead of the second-place Philadelphia Phillies; the heart-pounding, incredible six-game victory over the Houston Astros in the National League Championship Series—all seemed to be in vain.

You couldn't believe 55,078 people could be so quiet.

The huge clock on the right-field scoreboard had moved past midnight, but nobody had left the stadium. They sat silently, too shocked, too heartbroken to move.

Out of the corner of my eye, I could see the Red Sox in the third-base dugout, all of them on the top step, ready to rush out onto the field to celebrate their championship.

As I stepped into the batter's box, one thought kept flashing through my mind. I didn't want to be the answer to a trivia question: who made the final out of the 1986 World Series?

• • •

I never planned on being a Major League Baseball player. If I entertained any lofty ambitions at all, it was to be a quarterback in the National Football League because as a little kid and all through high school my best sport was football. In my boyhood dreams, I was going to be the next Bart Starr or Joe Namath.

I had been born into an athletic family. My dad, Jim, never played organized sports, but he was very sports-minded. His one claim to fame was that growing up in Kentucky, he attended the same school as the great Dodgers shortstop Pee Wee Reese. Later, Dad moved to California and worked in the aviation industry as an inspector of parts with Hughes Aircraft and later with McDonnell Douglas. He was always very supportive of my older brother Gordon and me in our athletic endeavors, working with us to improve, teaching us fundamentals, and attending as many of our games as he could. He was my coach in Little League, Pony League, and American Legion.

My mom was the real athlete in the family. Growing up in Illinois, she was a great swimmer who won many awards and trophies at the YWCA and was a lifeguard on Lake Michigan.

My brother Gordy, four years my senior, was my role model and my boyhood hero. I tried to do everything he did, only I wanted to do it better. There was a sibling rivalry between us, a friendly competition. If he made all-league, I wanted to do the

> *I tried to do everything he did, only I wanted to do it better.*

same. If he was Player of the Year in the county, I wanted to be Player of the Year also. If he got a college athletic scholarship, I wanted a college athletic scholarship.

Gordy was a terrific baseball player. He was drafted in the second round of the June 1968 free-agent draft (also taken in that draft were Thurman Munson, Bobby Valentine, Greg Luzinski, Garry Matthews, and Bill Buckner) by the California Angels, who offered him a signing bonus of $50,000. The Vietnam War was going on and Gordy was draft eligible, so he turned down the Angels and decided to go to USC, where he played on two NCAA championship teams for Coach Rod Dedeaux. After his junior year he was selected by the San Francisco Giants in the supplemental draft and signed for $10,000, so going to college cost him $40 grand. Gordon played two years in the minor leagues, and then left baseball and went into the restaurant business.

My big brother's success in baseball may explain why I gravitated to football. Maybe I was afraid I wouldn't be able to measure up to Gordy's success in baseball. Maybe I just wanted to do my own thing.

In 1961, the Ford Motor Company originated the "Punt, Pass, and Kick Contest," a national competition that was endorsed by the National Football League. It was a great idea, but they made the minimum age too young. It was open to kids from six to 10 years old. Later, they moved it up and made it from eight years old to 13, but in 1961 my brother was 11 and he couldn't compete. I was seven, and I could.

I won in the seven-year-old division, and I was brought to Green Bay and recognized with the other winners at halftime of the 1961 NFL Championship Game between the Green Bay Packers and the New York Giants.

Fortunately, we didn't have to compete in the cold at Green Bay, but two years later I competed again as a nine-year-old and they had the finals on the field of the championship game between the Giants and the Chicago Bears at Wrigley Field. It was 25 degrees below zero that day and I was supposed to go on the field and compete. I was leading in points in my division after the kick and the punt categories; all I had to do was pass well enough to keep my lead and I would win the championship for the second time.

Picture this nine-year-old California kid who didn't have the proper warm clothing trying to throw a football in frigid Chicago. I was freezing. My hands were like ice and my little body was trembling from the cold. When I tried to throw a pass, I slipped on the frozen turf because I was wearing tennis shoes. The ball slipped out of my hand, and I ended up in second place.

Nevertheless, because I was the first winner to make it back to the finals, the Ford Motor Company brought me to New York to shoot a television commercial. My mother went with me to New York, and we visited the Statue of Liberty, the Empire State Building, and Coney Island. Then they took us to a football field to shoot the commercial. The great sportscaster Chris Schenkel was the commentator, and if you can find a copy of the commercial, probably on eight-millimeter film, you'll see little nine-year-old Gary Carter kicking a football and saying something silly to Schenkel like, "This is exciting."

I was on top of the world at age nine, a two-time national "Punt, Pass, and Kick Contest" finalist and a "television star," but three years later my whole world came crashing down: my mom contracted leukemia and died suddenly, still in the prime of her life.

Those were difficult days for a 12-year-old. I was frightened and lonely and finding it hard to understand why God had taken my mom away from me.

Those were difficult days for a 12-year-old. I was frightened and lonely and finding it hard to understand why God had taken my mom away from me.

The one good thing that came out of it was that I had to learn to be self-sufficient. I had to grow up in a hurry. My dad would leave for work before I woke up and my brother and I would have to fend for ourselves. Dad would always be home for dinner, and he was always prompt. My brother would make dinner, and I had my responsibilities around the house. Together, Gordy and I shared the household chores, helping each other to do the vacuuming, the cleaning, and the laundry. That's how I became so domestic and why I am somewhat obsessive compulsive as far as being organized. Fortunately, to help me through that rough period, I had my older brother and my dad, who was both father and mother. And I had sports, which pretty much dictated my life.

I played baseball, basketball, and football, and I had begun to get a pretty good local reputation, especially in football, when I entered Sunny Hills High School.

In my sophomore and junior years, *Parade* magazine chose me as one of the top high school quarterbacks in the country. Now I was being bombarded by offers to play football from colleges all over the country. I heard from Notre Dame, Dartmouth, Colorado, all the Pac 8 schools, the Arizona schools, the Washington schools, the

Oregon schools, and all the California schools—UCLA, USC, Stanford, Fresno State, San Diego State, San Jose State. Getting an athletic scholarship was important to me because my dad couldn't afford to send me to college. UCLA was the only school that would allow me to play both football and baseball, so that's where I decided to go.

By the time I was a senior in high school, I had reached my full growth of 6'2" and 198 pounds. I was the second biggest guy on my football team, and I was the quarterback. I wanted to play defense because I enjoyed contact and would have liked to play cornerback, safety, or linebacker, but my coach wouldn't allow it. I did all the punting and placekicking. If I played defense, I never would have left the field. Also, coach didn't want me to risk injury on defense because my value was offense and we had a chance to win a championship.

As luck would have it, I did get injured before the season even started. We were scheduled to play Lynwood High School in a Friday night scrimmage just before our season opener, and they were taking the scrimmage very seriously. We were in our practice gear, no numbers, no glitz, no glamour, and they came out in full regalia, wearing game uniforms like it was a big-time game.

In a scrimmage, each team gets 10 plays to move the ball. I was a rollout quarterback, and on our second play my fullback fell down, my halfback took out the tight end, and I was heading up the field when a lineman hit me from one side and a cornerback hit me from the other. I went down, and when I got up, I could feel my knee was loose. Something was wrong.

I played eight more plays after that and then I told the coach, "Coach, my knee's killing me. I don't know what it is, but it just doesn't feel right."

The coach didn't hide his disappointment.

"Oh, yeah," he said sarcastically. "My big senior captain let me down."

That night I iced my knee and went to bed. As I always did, I woke up early the next morning, a Saturday. I had a job at a local Texaco station, and I had to be there at 7:00 AM. But when I woke up to go to work, my knee was swollen and sore. Somehow, despite the pain and swelling, I managed to get through work and the weekend. On Monday, I went to an orthopedist and he said I had to have surgery. I had a tear of the medial collateral ligament.

When I told my coach what the doctor said, his response was, "Would you consider wearing a brace and running the shotgun?"

"Coach," I said. "I've got to think about my future."

"Coach," I said. "I've got to think about my future." The next day I had the surgery, and I was on crutches and in a cast for eight weeks. There went my senior year. Amazingly, UCLA didn't rescind my scholarship. They had seen what I could do in my sophomore and junior years, and they still wanted me.

I got back to health in time for the basketball season, and then I played baseball. I had a pretty good season in baseball, good enough to be named Orange County Player of the Year and Freeway League Player of the Year. I didn't hit for a high average, but I showed some power.

I still wasn't considered a prospect in baseball, however. All my college scholarship offers were for football, UCLA being the only exception. In fact, when I was a sophomore, Tommy Lasorda's daughter, Laura, who was a senior at Sunny Hills, told her father about me. The Dodgers sent a scout to check me out, but I never heard from them, so the scout must have turned thumbs down on me.

In Little League, Pony League, and American Legion, and my first two years in high school, I was a shortstop and pitcher. If I did any catching, it might have been an occasional game in Little League as a trial-and-error thing. In my junior and senior years, when I got bigger and stronger, I was moved to third base and first base, and I still pitched a little.

By then, a Montreal scout named Bob Zuk had started showing up at our games. One day he asked me, "Have you ever thought about catching?"

I told him I might have caught a game or two in Little League, but that was it. Bob said I should consider catching because it would be the quickest way to the major leagues. I was taken aback. Nobody had ever said anything to me about the possibility of playing in the major leagues. Sure, as a kid growing up in the Los Angeles area, I was a big Dodgers fan and I often dreamed of wearing a Dodgers uniform and playing in Dodger Stadium for my favorite team. But in those dreams, I was a shortstop, or a third baseman, even a pitcher. Never a catcher!

Until then, I never seriously thought about playing Major League Baseball. In my mind, my future was football. I had it all planned. I was going to go to UCLA to play quarterback. I would probably redshirt as a freshman, and then I would play four years as a quarterback, replacing Mark Harmon, the actor and son of the great Michigan All-American and Heisman Trophy–winner Tom Harmon, and run the wishbone offense for Coach Pepper Rodgers. But now a Montreal Expos scout had put another thought in my head.

Until then, I never seriously thought about playing Major League Baseball. In my mind, my future was football.

To my surprise, five days after I signed a letter of intent to go to UCLA, I was drafted by the Expos, and in the third round, no less. Zuk told me later that what he saw in me that others obviously didn't see was leadership qualities and a guy who could develop into a catcher. All of a sudden, I had options…and a dilemma. I thought school was important, and still do, but I had to seriously consider baseball.

I was torn between going to UCLA and signing with the Expos. If I went to college to play football and baseball became secondary, where would that leave me?

For one thing, the Expos were offering a signing bonus of $35,000, plus an additional $7,500 as an incentive to reach the majors, and that seemed like all the money in the world to me. The entire contract was for $42,500 if I made it all the way.

Another factor was that I really didn't know if I had a future in football. I didn't know if I was NFL material. A lot of people who saw me play said I could have made it in the NFL, but I wasn't sure. Another thing that entered into my decision was the torn ligament in my right knee that caused me to lose my senior year in high school. Common sense told me that the chances of injury are much greater in football than they are in baseball. It's a fact that professional football players have a shorter career expectancy than baseball players.

Complicating matters was the fact that I had met and fallen in love with the girl I knew I was going to marry, who now has been my wife for more than 30 years. Sandy Lahm, who also attended Sunny Hills High, was everything I cherished in a mate and everything I wanted in a wife. She was beautiful, sensitive, intelligent, kind, considerate, supportive, and a devout Christian. We had become high school sweethearts and had begun to talk about a life together.

If I went to UCLA, Sandy, who was planning to attend Fullerton College, and I would be able to stay together and plan our future. But if I signed with the Expos, that would mean we'd be separated for as *I was being pulled in opposite directions.* long as I was playing in the minor leagues, or until we could get married. I was being pulled in opposite directions. Sandy and I talked a lot about my decision, and as much as she wanted me to stay close to home, she never put pressure on me to go to UCLA. She encouraged me to do what I thought was best for me.

So, with Sandy's support and blessing, I signed with the Expos and got started on my career in baseball.

• • •

My decision, hard as it was, was made. I signed with the Montreal Expos, sadly kissed Sandy good-bye, and off I went to an Expos minicamp in Jamestown, New York, to launch my professional baseball career and learn how to be a catcher.

There were about a dozen catchers in camp and I was easily the worst of the lot as far as fundamentals and technique. The Expos had given me a D-grade arm because I had a football arm. I was a quarterback, and the technique of throwing a football is different from that of throwing a baseball. Also, the technique of throwing a baseball as a catcher is different from that of throwing it as an infielder or a pitcher. As a result, when I threw to second base from the catching position, the ball would sail to the right.

Among the catchers in camp was Michel Dion, who later left baseball and became the goaltender for the Pittsburgh Penguins, and a good one. I was immediately impressed with him as a catcher. He couldn't hit very much, and that's why he left baseball, but he was an excellent receiver. His fundamentals and technique were outstanding. He blocked everything and he moved well. There I was struggling to learn the position and how to move to block balls, and Michel was doing it all so effortlessly. I couldn't help wondering if I would ever be as good as Dion.

Fortunately, in Jamestown I encountered a coach named Bill McKenzie. I learned so much from him in such a short time, particularly how to shift and move in order to block balls. I worked hard. I'd go out early and practice what McKenzie taught me. Before long I could feel the improvement as I began to get more comfortable at the position.

After two weeks of minicamp, the Expos sent me to Cocoa Beach in the Gulf Coast Rookie League, where I played my first 18 games as a professional. I batted .239 with two home runs and nine runs batted in. The Expos then sent me to West Palm Beach in the Florida State League, a very good class A league. I got in 20 games and batted .320, which did wonders for my confidence.

When the Florida State League season ended, I was able to get home for a few days before turning around and heading back to Florida for the Instructional League. I was getting a crash course in catching, and I loved every minute of it. Once I started improving behind the plate and getting more comfortable with the idea, I realized catching was where I belonged.

I came to appreciate and understand that as the catcher you're the only player on the field who is involved in every pitch (except for the pitcher, of course, and he doesn't play every day). A catcher is the only player in foul territory, and he has the whole game in front of him. I came to love the mental part of the game, the challenge of studying hitters and their tendencies, where to pitch them and how to set them up. The thing I loved, and the thing I miss the most—it's hard to believe that I have been retired for more than 15 years now— is calling the game. I loved setting up hitters, getting into their heads, and watching them take a pitch right down the middle of the plate because they were looking for something else.

I came to love the mental part of the game, the challenge of studying hitters and their tendencies, where to pitch them, and how to set them up.

I loved catching. Was there more wear and tear on my body as a catcher? Absolutely. You suffer the grind from being in that crouched position and the vulnerability you have with collisions at home plate and taking foul tips on a good portion of your body. Still, it was the one position in baseball that gave me a similar feeling to playing football, which I also loved. You can stick your nose in there if a guy's trying to take you out with a slide. Through the years, I think I pretty much held my ground in that regard and did a good job of blocking the plate.

2

Hey, Kid

The voice of pitcher Mike Torrez, a seven-year major league veteran, came through loud and clear. I was the "kid," a still-wet-behind-the-ears, not quite 19-year-old rookie in my first major league camp with the Montreal Expos in the spring of 1973.

I had been a professional baseball player for less than a year, having signed with the Expos right out of high school the previous summer. My professional experience consisted of a few weeks playing for the Cocoa Beach Expos in the Florida Gulf Coast League, a call-up to the class A Florida State League for a few games, and a few weeks in the Florida Instructional League, which is all the name implies, a league designed to instruct young players and hone their skills after the regular season has ended. In my case, the purpose was to teach me the rudiments of catching, a position I had never played until I turned pro.

When I was invited to the Expos' Florida training camp in Daytona Beach in the spring of 1973, I was excited, nervous, frightened, intimidated, and very much in awe of the major leaguers surrounding me. Back then rookies were expected to treat veterans like royalty. We were to be seen and not heard and to speak only when we were spoken to, and I conformed to all of those requirements.

I had already started to gain a reputation on the field for my enthusiasm, which was overwhelming. Like a kid, I was running around like crazy, trying to prove myself. I couldn't get enough batting practice, couldn't get enough work on the field. I wanted to win every sprint.

One day a group of veterans—Torrez, Tim Foli, Ken Singleton, and Mike Jorgensen—asked me to join them at the Americana Hotel, where they were going to play cards. I wasn't allowed to play, but I was invited to watch and just hang out. I didn't realize they had a reason for wanting me there until Torrez asked (ordered?) me to get some ice cream. Like an obedient rookie, I dutifully went down the elevator and across the street, where there was an ice cream store with 31 flavors, and brought them back some ice cream. And I had to pay for the ice cream, even though I wasn't making as much money as the veterans. At least I was getting the major league per diem in spring training and big-league meal money, which was big time for a kid who had earned $500 a month and $5-per-day meal money in the minor leagues the previous season.

Because I was so young and because of my boundless, boyish enthusiasm on the field, the veterans all called me "Kid." In one way it was an endearing name, and in another it was a subtle put-down, as if to say, "Look at this guy, running around, hustling all over the place; he's like a little kid." In any event, the name stuck. As time went on, my teammates and opposing players never called me "Gary" or "Carter." It was always "Kid." I'm in my fifties, and, to this day, my former teammates and contemporaries still call me "Kid."

When I incorporated, it was under the name Kid 8, Inc. for anything I did in Canada and Kid 8 Worldwide, Inc. for anything I did outside of Canada. My Florida license plate reads "Kid 8."

Because I was so young and because of my boundless, boyish enthusiasm on the field, the veterans all called me "Kid."

The "8" was my uniform number for most of my major league career. When I reported for my first big-league spring-training camp with the Expos in 1973, hanging in my locker was No. 57. Obviously, when you're a rookie and you aren't expected to make the 25-man roster, they give you a high number. It didn't matter to me that I was wearing the number of an NFL linebacker. I was happy just to have a uniform.

I still had No. 57 when I went to spring training in 1974 and again when I was called up to the Expos for nine games at the end of that season. But when I reported to spring training in 1975, in my locker was uniform No. 8. I figured if they were assigning me such a low number, it was a pretty good sign that I was going to make the team.

That spring we had six highly regarded rookies in camp, and one of the six was Pete Mackanin, who came to the Expos in a trade with the Texas Rangers. In Mackanin's locker was uniform No. 5. Given a choice, that was the number I would have preferred because Johnny Bench wore No. 5 and people were already saying that Bench might be the greatest catcher of all time. Johnny became my role model. Who better to emulate than the guy being touted as the greatest catcher of all time? I never got to see Bill Dickey, Mickey Cochrane, Gabby Hartnett, Roy Campanella, or Yogi Berra. Carlton Fisk was coming along at that time, but he wasn't yet recognized in a class with Bench. So I tried to develop my style like Johnny and my hustle like Pete Rose.

That was the way I tried to play the game and to respect the game. Bench was recognized as the best at my position and Rose was "Charlie Hustle." It was because of Pete and the way he played that I sprinted to first and hustled down the first-base line to back up throws to first base. Bench watched me do that and said, "Kid, you're not going to be able to do that forever," and he was right.

When I made the All-Star team in 1975, Bench befriended me, and it was then that I found out that Johnny is as good a person as he was a catcher.

I guess I could have asked Mackanin to switch numbers with me so that I could have Bench's No. 5, but when you're a rookie you can't complain about the number you're assigned, especially if it's a low number.

As it turned out, it was fate that I got No. 8. I was born on April 8. I got married on February 8. We moved into our first home in California on November 8. And look at all the great players who wore No. 8. Carl Yastrzemski. Willie Stargell. Yogi Berra. Bill Dickey. Joe Morgan. Cal Ripken Jr. All Hall of Famers. So when I was assigned No.

8, I remembered all those things and figured it would be a lucky number for me, and it was.

• • •

My second professional season began in the class AA Eastern League with Quebec City, where I batted .253 and showed some power with 15 homers and 68 RBIs. I also was named Most Valuable Player in the Eastern League All-Star Game. The Expos thought that wasn't bad for a 19-year-old and moved me up to Triple A for eight games. When the season ended, I managed to get home for one day, and then I was off again, to play for the city of Caguas in the Puerto Rican Winter League, where I played with and against major leaguers and Triple A players. I was named Most Valuable Player of the Caribbean World Series, and I felt I really was on my way.

In 1974, I was moved up to play for Memphis in the Triple A International League, the last stop before the majors. Exuding confidence, I had a good year in Memphis, with a .268 average, and was second in the league to Jim Rice in home runs with 23 and RBIs with 83. That earned me a call-up for the final two weeks of the season to Montreal, where I got in nine games: six as a catcher, two in the outfield, and one as a pinch-hitter. I came to bat 27 times and got 11 hits for a .407 average, one home run, and six RBIs. And then it was back to Caguas to play winter ball in Puerto Rico.

Somehow, I managed to get home in time to get married on February 8, 1975. Because I was away, Sandy made all the arrangements and did a wonderful job. Our wedding in the First Presbyterian Church of Fullerton was a beautiful, evening, candlelit ceremony.

With spring training about to start, there was no time for a formal honeymoon, but Sandy was coming with me to Florida, and finally, after all those separations, we would be together during spring training.

Needless to say, I was excited and happy and filled with hope reporting to spring training. Not only was I expected (and expecting) to make the team, but also there was a great deal of talk that I was being groomed to take over as the Expos' number-one catcher. But when I walked into the clubhouse in West Palm Beach, manager Gene Mauch said, "Hey, how's my right fielder doing?"

What? Right fielder? I thought the Expos wanted me to be a catcher. For two and a half years in the minor leagues I was groomed to be a catcher, and then they threw me an outfielder's glove and wanted me to play a position I had never played before. What was going on?

The good news: I was going to be given an opportunity to play, no matter what position it was. Gene just felt I had a better chance of adjusting to a new position, and he wanted to get my bat into the lineup. No complaints, I just wanted to play.

At the time, the Expos' starting catcher was Barry Foote. The year before, as a rookie, he had batted .262 with 11 homers and 60 RBIs, and he had a great arm behind the plate. Mauch really liked Barry. He had come up through the minor leagues catching the Expos' young pitchers, and they felt comfortable with him. I needed experience. I still had so much to learn.

Well, all right, if the Expos wanted me to play the outfield, a position I had never played even in Little League, American Legion, or high school, I was willing. I just wanted to play. As it turned out, I played 92 games in the outfield, one at third base, and 66 at catcher. Foote caught 115 games. I batted .270 in my rookie season, with 17 homers and 68 RBIs, and was named The Sporting News National League Rookie of the Year and the Expos Player of the Year. Barry batted .194, hit seven homers, and drove in 30 runs, so I figured I would take over as the number-one catcher the following season. I might have, too, except for a series of mishaps and incidents not of my own making.

Well, all right, if the Expos wanted me to play the outfield, a position I had never played even in Little League, American Legion, or high school, I was willing. I just wanted to play.

The winter between the 1975 and 1976 seasons was the first time since I became a professional that I didn't play winter ball. It also was my first winter as a married man, and I put on quite a bit of weight as a result of Sandy's great home cooking. But I was only 22 years old ,and I figured there would be no problem losing the extra weight once spring training began.

Unfortunately, there was a lockout at the start of spring training, which set everybody back. Then I was hampered by a series of injuries that started in spring training when I was moved from right field to left because the multitalented Ellis Valentine was coming along, and the Expos wanted him to be their right fielder. Playing left field, I ran into a brick wall trying to catch a line drive off the bat of Boston's Dwight Evans and opened a gash in my forehead.

Later, also playing the outfield, I cracked two ribs robbing Dave Cash of a home run and broke my thumb running into teammate Pepe Mangual. And they say catching is dangerous!

I finished off the season with a broken right hand I sustained as a catcher in a collision with Sam Mejias during a rundown between third base and home. As a result, that season I played only 36 games in the outfield and 60 at catcher, batted only .219, hit six home runs, and drove in 38 runs. People were calling it the sophomore jinx.

That winter, I made up my mind that I would work hard and report to spring training in shape. I got into a workout program and starting lifting Nautilus. That's one of the big changes with today's major league players. In the old days, players weren't making a lot of money and many of them had jobs during the off-season, selling insurance or real estate, working as salesmen in clothing stores. They would report to spring training overweight and use the first few weeks of spring training to get into shape. After my first year in the minor leagues, I took a job working the graveyard shift in a bread factory, Bridgeford Foods. I made more money working in the bread factory than I did playing baseball that year.

Today's players make so much money, they don't have to work in the off-season. Many of them have personal trainers and they spend their winters working out, so they can report to spring training in shape.

When I went to spring training in 1977, I was in shape, I was healthy, and I was ready to compete with Foote for the number-one catcher's job. I had a great spring, and I was the Opening Day catcher. I hit a home run off Steve Carlton in the sixth inning that turned out to be the game-winning home run in a 4–3 victory. I was getting more playing time than Foote, which understandably displeased Barry. He asked to be traded, and the Expos accommodated him. On June 15, they sent him to the Phillies for pitcher Wayne Twitchell and I officially became the Expos' number-one catcher. I caught 146 games and started a streak of catching at least 138 games a season in eight of the next nine years.

Offensively, I had one of my best years, a .284 average, 31 homers, and 84 RBIs. The Expos finished fifth in the National League East that season, but it was just about that time we started coming together. The Expos had entered the National League as an expansion team in 1969, and for their first nine seasons, they finished last in a six-team division three times, fifth four times, and fourth twice. Now in 1977, although we finished fifth again, the Expos were building a powerful team with young players like Andre Dawson, Ellis Valentine, Larry Parrish, Warren Cromartie, Steve Rogers, Charlie Lea, Tim Wallach, Bill Gullickson, Scott Sanderson, and later, Tim Raines.

We finished fourth in 1978, moved up to second in 1979 and 1980, and in 1981, the year of the strike, we finished first in the second half and beat the Phillies in the playoffs for the division championship. We were young and talented, and we were convinced the Expos were going to be a National League power for the next four or five years.

Had it not been for the strike, I would have had a streak of nine straight seasons in which I played at least 141 games, six straight years with at least 20 home runs, and 11 straight years with at least 70 runs batted in. Nevertheless I put up pretty good numbers in that strike-shortened season. I hit 16 homers, drove in 68 runs in 100 games, won my second consecutive Gold Glove for defense and my first Silver Slugger Award (given to the player at each position who had the best offensive numbers), finished sixth in the National League Most Valuable Player voting, and was elected to the All-Star team for the fourth time.

I became the fifth player (the others were Arky Vaughan, Ted Williams, Willie McCovey, all in the Hall of Fame, and Al Rosen) to hit two home runs in an All-Star Game.

All professional athletes should have a man like Jerry Petrie in their corner, especially as their careers are winding down, to help them prepare for their life after sports.

I was only 27 years old and considered a mainstay for a contending team, so the Expos made me an offer I couldn't refuse. They wanted to talk about a long-term extension of my contract that would kick in with the 1983 season. I suggested they contact my Canada-based agent, Jerry Petrie. I trusted Jerry implicitly. He had become my best friend and the godfather to our daughter, Christy.

During my years in Montreal, Jerry had given me a tremendous amount of guidance. He was instrumental in setting up my financial portfolio for the future by leading me to the proper lawyers and financial advisers. All professional athletes should have a man like Jerry Petrie in their corner, especially as their careers are winding down, to help them prepare for their life after sports.

I found the Expos' offer very flattering. It was telling me they wanted me as a cornerstone for their future. Jerry had dealt mostly with hockey players, so we brought in Dick Moss to help with the negotiations.

Dick had been legal counsel for the Major League Players Association under Marvin Miller, but he had become a players' agent. We figured that because of his work with the union, he had knowledge of the inner workings of these negotiations, as well as a relationship with all baseball executives.

The previous year Dave Winfield had become baseball's first $2 million player when he signed a 10-year, $23 million deal with the Yankees as a free agent. While we realized that playing in Montreal was not quite like playing in New York, we figured that I was worth as much to the Expos as Winfield was worth to the Yankees. The Expos' offer was for seven years at approximately $2 million a year, a staggering amount for someone who, when I became a professional, thought it would be great if I could ever earn $100,000 a year playing baseball.

The decision I had to make was whether it would be wise to tie myself into a seven-year deal. The negative was that the way baseball salaries were escalating, after about three or four years, I probably could have commanded more than $2 million a year on the free-agent market (although I had no expectation that salaries would rise to the level they actually did reach). On the other hand, as a catcher, I knew the chances of injury were great, so accepting this seven-year offer was the safe way to go. It meant financial security for my family and me. At the time, we had two daughters, Christy, born in 1978, and Kimmy, born in 1980. Our son D.J. would come along in 1984.

We opted for the seven years and security.

Having made the long-term commitment to the Expos, several other changes occurred with the help of some sound advice from financial advisers and lawyers. It was advice that would put me in good stead in the future, down the road when my playing career was over and I had to decide what to do with the rest of my life to continue to support my family in the manner to which we had become accustomed. It's a problem that all professional athletes must face when their careers have ended, and perhaps some of them can learn from my experience. The professional athlete has a relatively short career span, a small window during which he is at his peak earning power. For instance, I played in the major leagues for 19 seasons and I made the All-Star team 11 times, but my peak earning power came in a seven-year period—seven years out of a 19-year career.

Most people enter the work force at about age 21 and continue to be productive until the age of 65 and beyond. Because professional athletes are often out of the game by age 40 or 45, they have to plan for a lot more years of retirement. I know what you're thinking: most people don't earn $2 million a year at the peak of their careers. How about those who do? People like Bill Gates and Warren Buffett and George Steinbrenner? How about radio and television stars like Katie Couric, Dan Rather, Jay Leno, David Letterman, Tom Brokaw, Don Imus, and Walter Cronkite, who can do their thing into their sixties, seventies, and eighties?

How about Frank Sinatra, who was a star in his twenties and was still commanding big money into his eighties? Or Garth Brooks and Elton John? How about Dustin Hoffman, who became a star with *The Graduate* in 1967, won an Academy Award with *Rain Man* 21 years later, and is still commanding big dollars today, 40 years after he started?

But no matter how much money they made or how many years they played, they all face the same questions, doubts, and anxieties I did when my career ended.

Consider also that most Major League Baseball players will never make the All-Star team. Few will play 19 seasons in the major leagues, and few will ever get a seven-figure salary. But no matter how much money they made or how many years they played, they all face the same questions, doubts, and anxieties I did when my career ended. So it behooves them to take the necessary precautions and provide for their future while they can. Today's modern pay scale is a little different with a chance to make a lot more money, but you still have to be smart and plan for the future.

In my case, playing in Canada, I had to pay 10 percent more in taxes than I would have if I played in the United States because I was responsible for provincial and federal taxes in Canada plus state and federal taxes in the United States. To offset the tax implications, I was advised to get into registered retirement plans. To do that, we had to become landed immigrants and full-time residents, which we did.

I not only bought a home in Montreal, but I also took a Berlitz course to learn some French. I got involved in local charities and showed up at many civic functions in and around Montreal. I made a full-time commitment that Montreal was going to be our home.

As a by-product, I found that people appreciated my efforts and my popularity in Montreal was at an all-time high. If there was an identity to a player among the people of Montreal, it was Rusty Staub, "Le Grande Orange," who had been traded 10-years earlier, and me.

In 1981, they changed all the tax laws in Canada. Registered retirement plans and deferred profit sharing plans were no longer allowed, so my lawyers and tax consultants suggested I move to a nontaxable state, and that's when we moved to Florida, near the Expos' training headquarters at the time in West Palm Beach.

After signing the seven-year contract, I truly thought I was going to play my entire career in Montreal. I thought I was going to be there forever. However, what I learned was that in baseball, as in life, nothing is forever.

3

The Trade

I WASN'T EVEN HALFWAY THROUGH THE FIRST YEAR OF my seven-year contract extension in 1983 when I began to hear the rumblings.

In 1982, I had had a terrific season with a .293 batting average, 29 homers, and 97 RBIs, and another Gold Glove, but the Expos finished a disappointing third in the National League East.

In 1983, my average slipped to .270, my home runs to 17, and my RBIs to 79, but I was suffering with tendinitis in my left elbow. The pain was so excruciating, I had to take cortisone shots just to be able to play through the pain. Again, the Expos finished in third place and I began to hear comments that I was not a winner.

Not a winner? I probably should have spent some time on the disabled list. Most guys wouldn't even have played with the pain I was feeling.

By 1984, even Expos owner Charles Bronfman got into the act. Bronfman wasn't a baseball man. His money came from his family business, Seagram's whiskey, and he thought he could run his baseball team like a distillery.

Even though he was the one who had to authorize my seven-year extension for $14 million, he didn't like the way things were going in baseball and the way salaries were getting out of hand. It was apparent that he was regretting giving me the contract, even though I had a huge year—a .294 average, 27 homers, a league-leading 106 RBIs, and my seventh All-Star selection. But the Expos finished fifth, and Bronfman was making remarks similar to one made by Branch Rickey in the fifties.

Rickey had been running the Pittsburgh Pirates, which, at the time, was the worst team in baseball. In 1952, the Pirates finished last in the eight-team National League for the second time in three years. About the only gate attraction they had was Ralph Kiner, who led the National League in home runs in each of his first seven seasons. Pirates fans—the few who attended games—would sit through these horrible performances just to see Kiner hit. After Kiner batted for what the fans figured was the last time in the game, and with the Pirates hopelessly behind, the fans would get up and leave the stadium in droves.

After hitting a league-leading 37 homers in 1952, Kiner asked Rickey for a raise and was told, "We finished last with you, we can finish last without you."

The next year, Kiner was traded to the Cubs.

That, it was becoming clear, was the attitude Bronfman had toward me—the Expos finished fifth with me, they could finish fifth without me—and he told general manager John McHale to unload my contract.

While the Expos were fielding trade offers for me from other teams, I was in a good position, holding a trump card.

I was a 10-and-five man (10 years in the major leagues, five with the same team), which meant I had the right to veto any trade. If I was going to go anywhere, it would have to be someplace I approved, but I knew the Expos were limited to the number of teams that would have the players to satisfy the Expos and would also be willing and able to pick up my contract, a prime requisite for the Expos in any trade.

In December I got a call from McHale, who said he had a deal in place and it was contingent on my approval. When a player gets traded, he wants to know two things: (1) Where am I going? and (2) Who are you getting for me?

The answer to number one was the New York Mets, which surprised me because I never thought the Expos would trade me to a team in their division.

The answer to number two was Hubie Brooks, a fine young infielder who was the key man in the deal for Montreal, and three prospects: Herm Winningham, an outfielder; Floyd Youmans, a pitcher; and Mike Fitzgerald, a catcher.

I had mixed emotions about the trade. One was that I felt betrayed. I had done everything I could with the idea that I would play my entire career in Montreal; I bought a home there, even built a home there, got involved in civic and charitable events in that city, and learned to speak the language.

> *I had mixed emotions about the trade.*

On the plus side, by the Mets picking up my contract, I actually was getting a raise because I wouldn't have to worry about the Canadian taxes any longer, and I knew the Mets were a team on the rise.

Like the Expos, the Mets were an expansion team. They came into the National League in 1962 and, for the first seven years of their existence, they finished 10th five times and ninth twice. Then, in 1969, they shocked the baseball world when they were "the Miracle Mets," winning the National League pennant and then beating the heavily favored Baltimore Orioles in the World Series.

For the next eight years, the Mets were contenders, until 1977, when they fell on hard times again. In 1980, the Mets brought in Frank Cashen, who had built the Orioles into an American League powerhouse, and charged him with doing the same for the Mets. He started by building up the farm system and supplementing the roster with some shrewd trades. Four years later, Cashen's program began to pay dividends when the Mets finished second under manager Davey Johnson.

Up from the farm system were exciting young players like Darryl Strawberry, Mookie Wilson, Lenny Dykstra, Kevin Mitchell, Wally Backman, and Kevin Elster, along with pitchers Dwight "Doc" Gooden, Rick Aguilera, and Roger McDowell.

Cashen augmented that group with some great trades. He got Ron Darling from the Texas Rangers in 1982, Sid Fernandez from the Dodgers and Keith Hernandez from the Cardinals in 1983, Ray Knight from the Astros in August 1984, and Howard Johnson from the Tigers on December 7, 1984, three days before the Mets made the trade for me.

The idea of going from a small-market team like the Expos to a large-market team in New York, the media capital of the world, kind of overwhelmed me. But I saw it as a tremendous opportunity, going to a team that I thought was on the verge of winning a world championship.

Despite my trepidations about playing in New York, as it turned out, going to the Mets was the best thing that could have happened to me at that time in my career.

Starting out, I was well received by the fans, the media, and my new teammates. It got around that management was bringing me in as an experienced catcher to handle their excellent, but young, pitching staff. The press was hailing my arrival as the final piece of the puzzle, but really I was just a small part of the winning ways.

The press was hailing my arrival as the final piece of the puzzle, but really I was just a small part of the winning ways.

First impressions are often lasting ones. We opened the 1985 season at home against the Cardinals on April 9, a cold, gray, and dreary day. In my first at-bat, I got hit on the elbow by a fastball from Joaquin Andujar. If it had happened sometime during the season, I probably would have left the game because the elbow swelled up immediately. I tried putting ice on it, but it was so cold, all I needed to do was stick my arm out in the air.

Because it was Opening Day, I stayed in the game. In the sixth inning I hit a double, and I went into second base with a headlong dive, which I always did. But this was the first time I had done that as a Met, and the fans, a capacity crowd of 46,781, went nuts. They loved it.

We jumped out to a 5–2 lead after six innings with Doc Gooden breezing. But then the Cardinals scored two in the seventh and one in the ninth, and we went into the tenth tied, 5–5.

In the bottom of the tenth I was scheduled to bat second. Keith Hernandez struck out, and I came to bat against Neil Allen, who had been traded by the Mets to the Cardinals for Hernandez. He threw me a curveball for ball one. I figured he would throw me another curveball because why would he throw me a fastball behind in the count? Sure enough, he threw another curveball, and I just sat on it and put a good swing on it.

I thought it was a no-doubter. As I started to go down to first base I was watching the flight of the ball, ready to raise my arm. I thought I smoked that ball, but the cold weather and the heavy air held it up. Lonnie Smith, the left fielder, jumped and almost came down with it. The ball barely cleared the fence. I don't know how much it cleared by, but it wasn't a lot.

I believe that was the first time at Shea Stadium a player was called out by the fans to take a curtain call.

The fans went absolutely ballistic. I came around home plate, and the whole team was there, waiting for me. I still remember the excitement and the fans going wild because I had just hit a walk-off home run to beat the Cardinals. I believe that was the first time at Shea Stadium a player was called out by the fans to take a curtain call.

After the homer, I did a few radio and television interviews, and I could hear in the background the fans, as they were leaving through the turnstiles, chanting, "Gar-ee, Gar-ee, Gar-ee." I was thinking I could remember hitting three home runs for Montreal in a game against Jim Rooker in 1977, which was a big deal at the time, and all I got from the fans was polite applause. You could barely hear the cheers after the third home run.

I learned right away that New York was going to be different. I was now playing for a special breed of fans. It was exciting to be a part of something very special. If hitting a walk-off home run in your first game with a new team is not special, I don't know what is.

It was exciting to be a part of something very special. If hitting a walk-off home run in your first game with a new team is not special, I don't know what is.

My first season in New York was a memorable one and an indication that the Mets were on their way. We won 98 games, eight more than the previous year, and pulled 2,751,437 fans into Shea Stadium, almost a million more than the previous season. I had a very good year. I batted .281, led the team in home runs with 32 and RBIs with 100, and felt I had a large part in helping the Mets contend for a division title right down to the final two days of the season.

We were three games behind the Cardinals when we went to St. Louis for a three-game series on October 1. We won the first game, 1–0, in 11 innings on a laser shot by Darryl Strawberry that struck the clock above the bleachers in right-center field. In the second game, Gooden struck out 10, and we won again, 5–2. Now we were only one game behind.

With a chance for a sweep that would have tied us with the Cardinals for first place, we trailed 4–3 going into the ninth inning. Our first two batters were retired, but Hernandez kept our hopes alive with a bloop single over short. I came up to bat with a chance to give us the lead, or a tie, or at least keep the inning alive for Strawberry. Cards manager Whitey Herzog brought in reliever Jeff Lahti to face me, and I gave him a battle, fighting off several pitches until I swung at a pitch up and in and punched it to right field. For a moment, I thought it might drop in and keep the inning alive, but right fielder Andy Van Slyke got a good jump and made the catch.

I was crushed. I hate making the last out in a game. But we had taken two out of three from the Cardinals and were still only two games out with three to play.

We went home for a three-game weekend series against, of all teams, the Expos, while the Cardinals hosted three against the Cubs. We both won on Friday night, so we remained two games behind the Cardinals with two games left. We still had a chance to finish in a tie for first place, but it would take us winning our final two games and the Cardinals losing their final two. Not a likely scenario.

On Saturday, we lost to the Expos and the Cardinals beat the Cubs, and it was over. There was no wild-card in those days. If there had been, we would have been in the playoffs. Instead, we prepared to go home.

Even though we were eliminated, 31,890 fans showed up for the final game of the season. Davey Johnson didn't play most of the regulars, and we lost the game, but the fans nevertheless stayed to the bitter end. It was their way of saying "thank you" for giving them such an exciting season.

The Mets reciprocated in kind. Frank Cashen came up with the idea of showing a video of highlights from the season on the huge message board in left-center field. When the video ended, more than 30,000 Mets fans were on their feet, cheering and applauding, which prompted a few players to go out on the field to acknowledge the applause. The next thing you knew, the whole team was out there, and then Wally Backman reached up and pulled off his Mets cap and flung it into the stands. Soon every player was doing the same thing.

The fans loved it. They cheered and cheered and it was obvious they were not only saying "thank you"; they were telling us they couldn't wait for next year.

Neither could we.

4

Magic: The 1986 NLCS

IF EVER THERE WAS A MAGICAL YEAR, IT WAS 1986 FOR the New York Mets. After the way we played the year before, we arrived in spring training with a great deal of confidence for the season. We started off by winning our first two games, losing the next three, and then running off an 11-game winning streak that included a four-game sweep of the Cardinals in St. Louis on April 24, 25, 26, and 27.

That set the tone for the season. On May 1, we led the National League East by five games. On July 1, our lead was 9½ games. On August 1, it was 15½, and we finished 21½ games in front of the Phillies.

A few days after the end of the 1985 season, I had had arthroscopic surgery to repair cartilage in my right knee. I wanted to get it done early so that I would be ready for spring training, and I was. My batting average dropped 26 points to .255, but I maintained my power numbers, 24 home runs and 105 RBIs, third in the league.

The surprising thing is that we had no other player with 100 RBIs, none with 30 home runs (Darryl Strawberry led the team with 27), only two .300 hitters (Keith Hernandez at .310 and Wally Backman, a platoon player, at .320), and no pitcher with 20 wins, and still we won 108 games. We did it with pitching, defense, and by doing the little things—moving runners along, playing hit-and-run—by employing sound fundamentals, with consistency, and solid contributions from everyone, including our role players.

We had seven players in double figures in homers, seven with at least 43 RBIs, seven who batted at least .277, six pitchers with double figures in wins, and two relievers (Roger McDowell and Jesse Orosco) with at least 21 saves.

What followed was one of the best championship series ever played, highlighted by a climactic Game 6 that many have called the greatest baseball game ever played.

While we coasted in the NL East, the Houston Astros did likewise in the West; two teams that entered the National League together as expansion franchises in 1962 paired up for the right to go to the World Series in 1986.

What followed was one of the best championship series ever played, highlighted by a climactic Game 6 that many have called the greatest baseball game ever played.

The series started in Houston and, for the Mets and their fans, it started badly. But if you were a baseball purist, it was a classic.

The pitching matchup was a beauty. For the Mets it was Dwight Gooden, who at the age of 21 had already won 58 games and struck out 744 batters in his first three seasons. The previous season he had been phenomenal with a record of 24–4, 268 strikeouts, eight shutouts, and an earned-run average of 1.53. He led the league in wins, ERA, innings pitched, and strikeouts and was the winner of the National League Cy Young Award.

Starting for the Astros was Mike Scott, the 1986 National League Cy Young Award winner with a record of 18–10, a league-leading 2.22 earned-run average, five shutouts, and 306 strikeouts. Ironically, the Mets had traded Scott to the Astros after the 1982 season, and he turned his career around after an encounter with Roger Craig, the guru of the split-fingered fastball.

Craig taught Scott the pitch, and Mike's career took off from there, but the word around the National League was that Scott's success was not due to the split-fingered fastball alone. When Scott pitched a no-hitter against the Giants on September 25, a reporter, realizing that we would be facing him in the National League Championship Series, asked me my opinion of him as a pitcher. My response was an honest one. Too brutally honest, it turned out.

"It's the general consensus around the league that Mike Scott cheats," I said.

I was speaking from experience, up close and personal. I had caught Mike in that year's All-Star Game and I remembered him striking out Jesse Barfield on a pitch that moved unlike any split-fingered fastball I had ever seen or caught. The ball veered and dipped in such a way and did the kind of tricks that were physically impossible without some extraneous help.

I couldn't pinpoint exactly what Scott was doing—scuffing the baseball, cutting it, nicking it, applying a foreign substance to it—but I knew he was doing something, and that something was illegal. As great as his split-finger was, it didn't make the ball move the way Scott's ball was moving.

Here was a guy who, when he pitched for the Mets, had a very straight fastball and who went from striking out 137 batters in 1985 to 306 strikeouts the next season.

Naturally, my comment got back to Scott, and that probably gave him some added incentive against us.

> *Whether he did it legally or illegally, Scott made me eat my words in the first game of the NLCS by striking me out three times.*

I don't want to take anything away from Scott's pitching that season or in that NLCS. He was phenomenal. He had reinvented himself into an outstanding pitcher and that took more than simply throwing an illegal pitch.

Whether he did it legally or illegally, Scott made me eat my words in the first game of the NLCS by striking me out three times. He also struck out Keith Hernandez three times and Ray Knight and Darryl Strawberry twice. He struck out 13 batters and held us to five hits, one each by Hernandez, Strawberry, Lenny Dykstra, Rafael Santana, and pinch-hitter Danny Heep.

Gooden was almost as good, but not quite. He allowed just seven hits, but one of them was a home run by Glenn Davis in the second inning, and that was the only run of the game.

As if going down one game to nothing wasn't bad enough, we had the unpleasant task in Game 2 of facing Nolan Ryan, who would become baseball's all-time strikeout king and the author of seven no-hitters. At 39 years old, Ryan, in 1986, was still an overpowering and dominant pitcher who had won 12 games for the Astros.

Nolan started Game 2 blazing. He retired the first nine batters in order, five on strikeouts. It looked like we were in for another tough day. But in the fourth, Wally Backman singled with one out, and Keith Hernandez followed with a single. I came to bat with runners on first and second and one out and drove a line drive to center that fell for a double, scoring Backman with the first run of the game. Strawberry followed with a sacrifice fly, and we had broken through for two runs against Ryan, our first two runs of the series after 12 consecutive scoreless innings.

In the fifth, we scored again. Singles by Santana and Dykstra, an RBI single by Backman for one run, and a triple by Hernandez for two more runs and we were up, 5–0.

After that, Bobby Ojeda took over. He pitched brilliantly. He allowed 10 hits, but he got the big outs when he needed them, stranded nine base runners, and went all the way for a 5–1 victory that tied the series. And for the next three games we were going back to Shea Stadium, where we would have the advantage of those wild and wonderful Mets fans behind us.

Game 3 featured one of those miraculous comebacks and sudden-death finishes that would come to be a Mets trademark in that postseason. Ron Darling started the

Game 3 featured one of those miraculous comebacks and sudden-death finishes that would come to be a Mets trademark in that postseason.

game for us, and the Astros jumped on him for two runs in the first and two in the second. Meanwhile, veteran left-hander Bob Knepper had held us to four singles over the first five innings. But in the sixth, we attacked. Singles by Kevin Mitchell and Hernandez and an error by shortstop Craig Reynolds on my ground ball brought in one run. Strawberry followed with one of his towering, majestic home runs to tie the score, 4–4.

In the seventh, the Astros regained the lead on an unearned run, and we came to bat in the bottom of the ninth trailing, 5–4. Backman led off with a bunt single and went to second on a passed ball. Heep batted for Santana and flied to center, and that brought up "little" Lenny Dykstra, who had entered the game as a pinch-hitter in the seventh. Lenny was small in stature, only 5'9", but he was strong and tough. That's why his nickname was "Nails."

And Nails nailed one, a tremendous drive over the right-field fence, a walk-off home run that gave us a dramatic sudden-death, come-from-behind, 6–5 victory. The place went bonkers: cheers, shouts, a curtain call for Lenny. We had taken a 2–1 lead in the series, and we were two wins away from going to the World Series. But we had to deal with Mike Scott in Game 4.

Just as he had done in Game 1, Scott tied us in knots with his split-finger and whatever else. He struck out only five but allowed just three hits, all singles, and beat us 3–1 to even the series.

We were convinced Scott was cheating, and to prove it, we collected two dozen baseballs from that game that all had a scuffmark in the same spot and sent them to National League president Chub Feeney for a ruling. Feeney said, "No, they hit the ground." Okay, no problem, we still had the home-field advantage for Game 5 and the opportunity to go up one game in front of our fans.

Game 5 was another classic, Nolan Ryan against Doc Gooden, and it would be a preview of what was still to come. Ryan was spectacular, vintage Nolan. And Doc was gritty.

Through nine innings, Gooden was touched up for eight hits but only one run, which was scored in the fifth when we failed to complete an inning-ending double play. Meanwhile, just as he had done in Game 2, Ryan retired our first nine batters and struck out six of us.

When Nolan is throwing like he was that day, the thought of a no-hitter is always in your mind. Going into the bottom of the fifth, he was working on a perfect game, 12 up, 12 down. I led off the inning with a fly ball to right, making it 13 up, 13 down. That brought up Strawberry, and he teed off on a Ryan fastball and blasted it out of the park to tie the score, 1–1.

That's how it remained through the ninth. In the top of the tenth, Ryan left for a pinch-hitter and was replaced on the mound by Charlie Kerfield, who was big and mean and threw hard. Gooden pitched the tenth and was replaced by Jesse Orosco in the eleventh.

Neither team scored in the eleventh. Orosco got the Astros in order in the top of the twelfth. With one out in the bottom of the twelfth, Backman singled off third baseman Denny Walling's glove, only our third hit of the game. With Hernandez at bat, Kerfield tried to pick Backman off first and threw the ball away. Wally took second. That forced Astros manager Hal Lanier to make a decision: pitch to Keith or walk him and go after me, righty against righty, hoping for an inning-ending double play.

Lanier opted for the latter, which I admit was the right thing to do. Besides, I was having a horrible series (1-for-21 to that point).

'Don't let them do this to you, Kid,' [Strawberry] said. 'Don't let them do it.'

As Kerfield was throwing four wide ones to Keith, I heard the voice of Darryl Strawberry coming from behind me.

"Don't let them do this to you, Kid," he said. "Don't let them do it."

I ran the count to 3-and-2 and fouled off a couple of pitches. The tension in the air was palpable. The crowd of almost 55,000 was buzzing in anticipation. Kerfield pitched and I caught it on the sweet spot, but I couldn't get any lift on the ball and it rocketed back to the mound. Kerfield stabbed at it. If he had been able to get his glove up in time, it would have been an easy, tailor-made double play, and we'd be going to the thirteenth. But the ball zipped past Kerfield's glove, over second base, and into center field.

Backman was off with the crack of the bat. He sailed around third and headed home. Center fielder Billy Hatcher charged the ball, scooped it, and came up throwing to the plate. A slide. A cloud of dust. And plate umpire Joe West signaled safe. Backman scored, the crowd went wild, and we had won the game, 2–1, taking a three-games-to-two lead in the series in the process.

Now it was on to Houston with a chance to clinch the National League pennant. All we had to do was win one out of two games.

If Game 5 was tense, tight, dramatic, and emotion-packed, it was nothing compared to Game 6 in the Astrodome on October 15. As I mentioned, many people have called it the greatest baseball game ever played. I don't know about that, but I do know it was the greatest game I ever played in.

It started as a duel of left-handers, Bobby Ojeda for us, Bob Knepper for Houston, and we immediately fell into a deep hole as the Astros scored three runs in the first inning. At that point, Ojeda settled in and kept us in the game by allowing just one hit through the fifth.

But we were doing nothing against Knepper, who was masterful. Through eight innings, we had only two hits off him, a single in the third by Santana and a single in the eighth by Tim Teufel.

As we came to bat in the top of the ninth, we still trailed, 3–0, and we were three outs away from having to face Mike Scott, who had already beaten us twice, in Game 7. Our dream season was in serious jeopardy.

To start the top of the ninth, manager Davey Johnson sent Dykstra up to bat for reliever Rick Aguilera, and Nails came through again, driving a shot past center fielder Hatcher that rolled all the way to the wall as Dykstra raced around the bases and slid into third with a triple. Mookie Wilson followed with a single to score Dykstra, and we had finally broken through against Knepper. Was it too little and too late?

Kevin Mitchell grounded to third and was thrown out for the first out of the inning. Fortunately, the ball wasn't hit hard enough for the Astros to turn a double play, which probably would have taken the heart out of us. Instead, we were still alive when Hernandez doubled Mookie home to make it 3–2. We had the tying run on second with only one out. We had life.

As I started to approach the batter's box, Astros manager Hal Lanier popped out of the Houston dugout and waved to the bullpen for Dave Smith, who had been the Astros' dominant, lockdown closer all season with four wins and 33 saves.

My at-bat was another one of those marathons, a full count and several foul balls to keep the at-bat going until Smith missed for ball four. Now we had the tying run on second and the go-ahead run on first with one out and Strawberry coming to the plate.

Darryl hit a towering drive deep to right field, a no-doubter. When it left the bat, everyone in our dugout jumped up to follow the flight of the ball, and the hearts of 45,718 Astros fans skipped a beat. But the ball went foul. The fans let out a sigh of relief, and the guys in our dugout sat down dejectedly.

Straw's shot, and his intimidating presence at the plate, may have scared Smith out of the strike zone—"bat shy," players call it. Smith wound up walking Darryl to load the bases for Ray Knight. Ray, a cool veteran and professional hitter, delivered a sacrifice fly to tie the score. We had done again what we did all season—come from behind in dramatic fashion. This was a team that wouldn't quit, that refused to lose.

The game went into extra innings. Even though we had a margin for error (if we lost, we still had another chance tomorrow), there was a sense of urgency for us. We knew that if we lost, the pitcher for the Astros the next day would be Mike Scott.

We knew that if we lost, the pitcher for the Astros tomorrow would be Mike Scott.

Roger McDowell, who had usually pitched no more than two innings during the season, came in to start the ninth inning and did a phenomenal job, holding the Astros to one hit over the next five innings. For Houston, Larry Andersen pitched the eleventh, twelfth, and thirteenth without allowing a hit, so we went to the fourteenth still tied, 3–3.

I led off the top of the fourteenth with a single and moved to second on a walk to Strawberry. Ray Knight, attempting to sacrifice the runners to second and third, bunted too hard, and I was forced at third. But Backman came through with a single to short right field, and Straw took a gamble, rounded third, and scored on a close play at the plate. We had our first lead of the game, and Jesse Orosco ready to nail it down.

But with one out in the bottom of the fourteenth, Billy Hatcher atoned for misplaying Dykstra's ninth-inning triple by driving one to left field that hit the screen on the fair side of the foul pole for a home run. The game was tied once more. Who said this was going to be easy?

On we went into the fifteenth and the sixteenth innings, both teams exhausted.

Strawberry got us started in the top of the sixteenth with a double, and Knight singled him in to give us the lead again. And we weren't finished. A couple of wild pitches scored Knight. A walk, a sacrifice, and a single by Dykstra and we had scored three times for a 7–4 lead. With Orosco on the mound, we had to think a three-run lead would be enough. Not in this game!

Before we knew it, we were in deep trouble. With one out, a walk and a pair of singles gave the Astros a run and put the tying runs on base. Our bullpen was depleted, so it was going to be up to Orosco to gut it out. Davey Johnson was going to do or die with Jesse.

Orosco stiffened and got a force-out, leaving us needing just one more out for the pennant. But Glenn Davis kept the Astros' hopes alive with a single to score Billy Doran and make it a one-run game. Nothing comes easy.

Now the Astros had the tying run on second, the winning run on first, and Kevin Bass coming to bat. Bass was a good fastball hitter, so I went to the mound to talk to Orosco and to pump him up. I told Jesse we were going to throw Bass nothing but sliders, and I also told him, "You're the best, J.O. I believe in you. I know you can do it."

Orosco threw five straight sliders to Bass. If Kevin had stood there with his bat on his shoulder, he probably would have walked, but the situation made him anxious. He swung at two sliders off the plate and missed them both, and he ran the count full. Five pitches, five sliders. Bass must have figured there was no way Orosco was going to throw him six straight sliders in the at-bat. Bass was wrong.

Jesse pitched, and Bass took a mighty swing...and missed.

It was over. After 16 innings, four hours, and 42 minutes, it was over. We were National League champions.

To a man, we were ecstatic on the outside, but on the inside we were physically and emotionally drained. And in less than 72 hours, we were going to have to face the Boston Red Sox in the World Series.

5

The Magic Continues:
The World Series

AFTER THE HARD-FOUGHT, TENSE, AND GRUELING
National League Championship Series with the Astros,
we were physically exhausted and emotionally drained.
But we were playing in the World Series, and, let's face
it, you never heard of any player ask for a day off in the
World Series because of fatigue.

In the World Series, you're going on adrenaline, excited
by playing on the big stage, and feeding off the energy of
the fans.

Our opponents, the American League champion
Boston Red Sox, had won their division by five games
and then beaten the California Angels in a seven-game
American League Championship Series that was just as
intense as ours. In so doing, the Red Sox showed the same
kind of grit and never-say-die attitude as we had. They
had fallen behind three games to one and had come back
to sweep the last three games to advance to the World
Series.

We knew the Red Sox would be tough. They had a powerhouse team that included Wade Boggs, the American

League batting champion with a .357 average; four hitters (Don Baylor, Dwight Evans, Jim Rice, and Bill Buckner) with 18 homers or more and at least 94 RBIs; and Roger Clemens, who had a record of 24–4, an earned-run average of 2.48, and had struck out 238 batters. The Red Sox offense was tailor-made for their home field, Fenway Park, with its cozy left-field wall called "the Green Monster."

If the Red Sox needed any additional incentive, their last World Series championship had come 68 years before.

If the Red Sox needed any additional incentive, their last World Series championship had come 68 years before.

The World Series opened in Shea Stadium on Saturday night, October 18, with the fans still feeling the euphoria—and the Mets players still with an emotional hangover—from the excitement of the victory over the Astros. Clemens, Boston's ace, had started the seventh game of the ALCS and our ace, Doc Gooden, had started the fifth game of the NLCS, so the starting pitchers in the World Series opener were left-hander Bruce Hurst for the Red Sox and Ron Darling for us.

Darling was outstanding. In seven innings, he allowed just three hits, struck out eight, and gave up a run in the seventh, which was unearned. It came without benefit of a hit.

Hurst was even better. He gave up four hits (I had one of the four, a meaningless broken bat single in the sixth), also struck out eight, and didn't allow a run. Calvin Schiraldi, who had been traded by the Mets to the Red Sox in a deal that brought Bobby Ojeda to New York during

Competing in Ford Motor Company's "Punt, Pass, and Kick Contest." As a kid, I always thought I'd play in the NFL.

With my mother, Inge, and longtime TV commentator Chris Schenkl at the commercial shoot in New York for the "Punt, Pass, and Kick" contest.

On the field with my wife, Sandy, during my rookie season in 1975. I was 21 years old, newly married, and embarking on my first year in the big leagues with the Expos.

I enjoyed playing for the Expos. Here I am with some fans in June 1983.

In 1985, I was traded to the New York Mets. This photo of Sandy and me was taken just after Opening Day. In my first game, I had a walk-off home run against the Cardinals. Not a bad beginning.

Eddie Milner steamrolling me on his quest to score a run.

A play at the plate with Rafael Palmeiro at Wrigley Field.

One of the fist pumps from a requested curtain call.

Celebrating our 1986 World Series victory on the field, immediately after winning Game 7.

Sandy and I riding through the ticker-tape parade after the Mets' 1986 World Series victory. The enthusiasm and love from the New York fans was truly wonderful.

A Father's Day advertisement for Bloomingdales that my three children and I did together, following up on my success with the Mets. Pictured from left to right are Christy, Kimmy, and D.J.

In 1992, I went back to Montreal to play for the Expos. From left to right, Christy, Sandy, D.J., me, and Kimmy, pose on Family Day.

I retired in 1992, at age 37, after one last year with the Expos.

In 2000 I started the Gary Carter Foundation, whose brochure is pictured here. The foundation has raised $8 million to fight leukemia and also gives financial support to nine schools in underprivileged areas.

Pictured here with me are two of the kids I support through the foundation: Chloe Texter and Franklin Ocean. If you want to learn more about the foundation, go to www.garycarter.org

the previous winter, pitched a scoreless ninth and the Red Sox took Game 1, 1–0. If we had any consolation, it was that we had also lost Game 1 of the League Championship Series, and by the same score, and still came back to win.

In Game 2 the fans, and the television network, got the pitching matchup they wanted, Roger Clemens against Doc Gooden. As so often happens when there is a much-anticipated pitching matchup, this one was a dud. Gooden was pounded for six runs and eight hits and left after five innings. Clemens was removed in the fifth when we rallied to cut the lead to 6–3. We ended up losing the game, 9–3.

We had lost the first two games at home and had to go to Boston for the next three games. In the papers the next day, a lot was made of the fact that no team, aside from Kansas City, had ever lost the first two games at home and come back to win the World Series. We disregarded those stories (we had overcome odds and obstacles all season; there was no reason we couldn't do it again), and the rallying cry in our clubhouse was, "Let's not lose this World Series in Boston; let's at least bring it back to New York and take our chances."

Game 3 was scheduled for Tuesday, October 21, with Monday a day off for travel. We were supposed to work out in Fenway Park on the day off, but manager Davey Johnson made a decision that might have been the turning

In the papers the next day, a lot was made of the fact that no team, aside from Kansas City, had ever lost the first two games at home and come back to win the World Series.

point in the Series. He canceled the workout and told us to take the day off and rest. My wife, Sandy, and I stayed in our hotel room the entire day. We ordered room service and relaxed as I attempted to recharge my body for the grueling days that were ahead.

Did the day off help us in Game 3? We'll never know. What we do know is that we came out swinging against Dennis "Oil Can" Boyd and put four runs on the board in our first chance at bat. Lenny Dykstra, who had started so many rallies and had become our catalyst, started the game with a home run. Wally Backman and Keith Hernandez singled, and I followed with a double for our second run. Danny Heep then singled to drive in two more.

Ojeda, no doubt hyped by pitching against the team that had traded him away, was outstanding for seven innings, allowing one run and five hits, and we took Game 3, 7–1. Things were looking much better for the New York Mets.

One game can shift momentum and turn things around in a seven-game series, and we felt that's exactly what we did by winning Game 3. Davey Johnson's ploy to skip a workout on the off day paid off. We were brimming with confidence for Game 4, convinced we had turned a corner.

Ron Darling started for us against Al Nipper and the game was scoreless going into the top of the fourth when Wally Backman led off with a single and moved to second on an infield out. I came to bat against Nipper, who had struck me out looking with a 3–2 slider in the first. I filed that at-bat in my mind, and I knew Nipper did, too. I was not going to let him do it to me again.

I figured Nipper was thinking I would be looking for the slider again, and he would try to fool me by throwing a fastball. Those are the kinds of mind games that go on with a pitcher and catcher against a hitter—the part of the game I loved so much.

This time I figured right. Nipper threw me a fastball and I was waiting for it. I crushed it into the screen above the Green Monster in left field to give us a 2–0 lead. As I rounded the bases, I couldn't help thinking of all the baseball legends who had hit home runs in this historic ballpark: Ted Williams, Carl Yastrzemski, Joe DiMaggio, Mickey Mantle, Jimmie Foxx, and the incomparable Babe Ruth.

I led off the sixth with a double off Nipper and was stranded, but Darling was hanging up zeros on the scoreboard and we plated two in the seventh on Lenny Dykstra's two-run homer. When I came to bat in the eighth, we were leading 5–0.

Steve Crawford was now pitching for the Red Sox. On a 0–2 count, he hung a curveball, and I jumped all over it and drove it toward the Green Monster, over the Monster, over the screen, and onto Lansdowne Street. I had hit two home runs in a World Series game. You could count on the fingers of two hands the players who had done that. We won the game, 6–2, and drew even with the Red Sox at two games each. Now it was a best-of-three series.

The game of baseball is such a roller-coaster ride. There's an old adage that you can never get too high or

The game of baseball is such a roller-coaster ride. There's an old adage that you can never get too high or too low, and I was living proof of that in the World Series.

too low, and I was living proof of that in the World Series. One night, I hit two home runs and a double in a game, the next I came to bat four times and couldn't get the ball out of the infield.

That was Game 5, won by the Red Sox, 4–2, as Bruce Hurst stymied us again. He was becoming the Red Sox's Mike Scott.

Losing Game 5 was a big disappointment. It meant we would have to win the next two games to be world champions. But at least we had accomplished our goal of bringing the Series back to Shea Stadium and we would have our home fans with us in those final two games. That was the good news. The bad news was the starting pitcher we would be facing in Game 6—Clemens.

The day before Game 6 was a travel day. Once again, Davey Johnson chose to eschew the customary workout as he did before Game 3.

Game 6 on Saturday night, October 25, was one of the most memorable, most talked about World Series games ever played, and it wasn't turning out well for the Mets in the early going. The Red Sox reached Bobby Ojeda for single runs in the first and second innings, and through the first four innings, we didn't get anything close to a hit off Clemens, who was throwing aspirin tablets. He had already racked up six strikeouts.

In the fifth, we finally broke through. Clemens walked Strawberry, who stole second and scored on Ray Knight's single. Mookie Wilson followed with a single to right, and Knight went to third when the usually sure-handed Dwight Evans bobbled the ball. Knight scored when Danny Heep rapped into a double play, and the score was tied, 2–2.

Roger McDowell relieved Ojeda in the seventh and gave up the lead on an unearned run. We were down by a run to Clemens and had only nine outs remaining. Roger retired the side in order in the seventh, but when we came to bat in the eighth, for some inexplicable reason, Clemens was gone and Calvin Schiraldi was on the mound. No knock on Schiraldi, but Clemens is Clemens, and we were happy to see him out of the game.

The first batter Schiraldi faced, pinch-hitter Lee Mazzilli, singled, and we had a ray of hope. Dykstra was signaled to sacrifice Maz to second and he laid down a good bunt, which Schiraldi fielded. He tried for a force at second but bounced his throw, and both runners were safe. Backman sacrificed the runners to second and third. With first base open, Boston manager John McNamara elected to walk left-handed-hitting Keith Hernandez to load the bases and try for the inning-ending double play with me coming up.

I had a momentary flashback to Game 5 of the NLCS, and the similarities were eerie—Nolan Ryan, a power pitcher just like Clemens, starting for the Astros, then leaving prematurely, to be replaced by a big, hard-throwing right-hander, Charlie Kerfield, just like Schiraldi. And then, in the twelfth inning, with a runner on second, Kerfield gave Hernandez an intentional walk to pitch to me, looking for a double play. I remembered what Straw had said to me in Houston: "Don't let them do this to you, Kid."

All those things, so similar to this time, came back to me as I stepped up to the plate against Schiraldi, who suddenly had trouble throwing strikes. His first three pitches were out of the strike zone. I was up in the count, 3–0. One more ball would force in the tying run.

Automatically, I looked down at third-base coach Bud Harrelson, thinking he would surely give me the "take" sign on 3–0. To my surprise, and my glee, Buddy was giving me the sign, relayed from manager Davey Johnson, to swing if I liked the pitch.

> *The next pitch might have been ball four. I wasn't going to wait to find out.*

"Wow! The green light on a 3–0 pitch. That's like a glorified 2–0 pitch. You just make sure you put a good swing on the ball," I thought.

The next pitch might have been ball four. I wasn't going to wait to find out. It was good enough to hit, and I put a good swing on it and drilled it on a line to left field. It was hit hard, but right at Jim Rice, who made the catch. But it was deep enough for Mazzilli to score from third, tying the game at 3–3.

Rick Aguilera had come in to pitch the ninth, which he got through unscathed despite an error by shortstop Kevin Elster. Against Schiraldi in the bottom of the ninth, we put our first two runners on with a walk and a throwing error by catcher Rich Gedman on a bunt by Mookie. Two runners on, nobody out, a chance to win the game right there...until a strikeout and two fly outs ended the threat. We were going into what was becoming familiar territory: extra innings.

Our spirits sagged when Dave Henderson led off the top of the tenth with a home run into the left-field seats. It's only one run, I told myself. We've come back so many times from a one-run deficit to win, we could do it again. But then it was a two-run deficit when Wade Boggs doubled and Marty Barrett singled him home, and things, to put it mildly, looked bleak.

When Wally Backman, one of our catalysts, started the bottom of the tenth with a fly ball to left and Keith Hernandez hit a ball to deep left-center field that was caught by Dave Henderson, it looked like we were done. In their dugout, the Red Sox were whooping it up.

After flying out, Hernandez was so disgusted, he angrily stormed off the field and into the clubhouse. He wasn't going to sit in the dugout and watch us lose. In the clubhouse, he threw his glove into his locker, grabbed a beer, lit a cigarette, and sat in Davey Johnson's office watching the end of the game on television.

Two outs, nobody on base in the bottom of the tenth inning: we were one out away from the end of our season, and a great season it had been, a dream season.

It couldn't end like this, could it?

Our fans, those crazy, loyal Mets fans, were still in their seats, God love them. They weren't conceding defeat, and neither was I, our last hope. I was determined not to make the final out of the World Series.

[The fans] weren't conceding defeat, and neither was I, our last hope.

I tried to think positively as I took my stance in the batter's box against Schiraldi, a former Met. We had been the cardiac kids all season. We had had so many come-from-behind wins, why not one more? All year, I always felt we were capable of coming back no matter how deep a hole we were in, and now we were in the deepest hole imaginable. We were a team that had a never-say-die attitude, a team that wouldn't quit, that refused to lose. What was it the great Yogi Berra said? "It ain't over 'til it's over."

The count went to 2-and-1. I knew Schiraldi had to be thinking he didn't want to walk me and bring the tying run to the plate, so he didn't want to run the count to 3–1. I knew he would come in with a fastball, and I was right.

Schiraldi's fastball came in nice and fat. I met it solidly and lined a single to left field. At that point, something strange happened that might have given us a wake-up call. I was so absorbed in the game and my at-bat that I didn't see it, but I found out later that just as my line drive dropped safely into left field, a message flashed briefly on the big Shea Stadium message board. Apparently whoever was operating the board inadvertently pressed the wrong button because what was flashed was a message congratulating the Red Sox on winning the World Series and Boston pitcher Bruce Hurst on being named World Series Most Valuable Player.

That message, and my single, seemed to energize the crowd. We were not dead yet.

Kevin Mitchell batted for Rick Aguilera and lined a single to center. Hope lives.

Ray Knight was next. He blooped one to center that fell in for a hit. I took off with the crack of the bat and scored, and Mitchell, the tying run, went all the way to third.

Now the crowd was going wild, sensing another miracle comeback as Red Sox manager John McNamara went to the mound and replaced Schiraldi with veteran Bob Stanley to pitch to Mookie Wilson.

With Mookie at bat, Stanley fired a pitch past catcher Rich Gedman to score Mitchell with the tying run, sending Ray Knight into 2nd with the winning run. You could sense the air come out of Boston's balloon as the crowd went berserk. We were alive.

The count on Mookie went to 3–2. On the next pitch, he hit an easy four-hopper to first baseman Bill Buckner, the simplest ground ball for any major leaguer. Buckner had been playing with a bad ankle that left him hobbling around unsteadily, and later McNamara would be second-guessed for not replacing Buckner on defense with Dave Stapleton, which he had done in three of the first five games of the World Series and throughout the last few weeks of the regular season. McNamara would later explain that the veteran Buckner had been such a vital part of the Red Sox's success that season, McNamara wanted him to be on the field when the Sox won their first World Series in 68 years. Sentiment got in the way of Johnny Mac's better judgment.

Wilson's bouncer trickled under Buckner's glove and into short right field as Knight came all the way around from second base to score the winning run as the fans and players went crazy in jubilation.

As excited as I was, I have to admit it was sad to see an outstanding player like Buckner, a true gamer who had such a great career, suffer such a devastating experience. He would have to live with it forever.

My sympathy for Buckner would have to be put on hold, however. I could feel sorry for his misfortune in the future. Right now, we had one more game to play, and after the way we came back in Game 6, we believed wholeheartedly that no matter how many runs we fell behind in Game 7, we were going to come back and win the World Series.

It rained on Sunday, October 26, and Game 7 was postponed. What effect that had on the two teams in Game 7 is difficult to say. It probably helped the Red Sox who were able to give their starting pitcher, Bruce Hurst, an extra day of rest. He would be pitching with three days' rest instead of two.

That extra day of rest seemed to work wonders for him. He retired us in order in four of the first five innings, while the Red Sox put up a three spot off Darling in the second, two of them on solo homers by Dwight Evans and Rich Gedman.

We broke through in the sixth after Hurst got the first out. He had retired 16 of our first 17 batters when Lee Mazzilli started a rally with a pinch-hit single. Mookie followed with a single, and Tim Teufel walked to load the bases. Hernandez singled in two runs, and I followed with a looper to right field. Evans tried for a shoestring catch and couldn't make it. He recovered in time to force Keith at second, taking a hit away from me. But I was credited with an RBI when the tying run scored on the play.

In the next inning, we exploded for three more runs against Calvin Schiraldi, who was having a terrible Series against his old team. In one-third of an inning, he gave up a home run to Ray Knight, singles to Dykstra and Rafael Santana, and uncorked a wild pitch before being relieved by Joe Sambito, who allowed a sacrifice fly to Hernandez. We had a 6–3 lead with two innings to go, but after what had happened in Game 6, we still didn't feel secure.

To their credit, the Red Sox showed what they were made of by battling back with two runs in the eighth before a man was out, cutting our lead to a slim one-run until Jesse Orosco came in to leave the tying run stranded at second base by retiring three straight batters. We put the game away with two runs of our own in the bottom of the eighth, one of them on a Darryl Strawberry home run off Al Nipper.

We had a 6–3 lead with two innings to go, but after what had happened in Game 6, we still didn't feel secure.

In the top of the ninth inning, roles were reversed. Now it was the Red Sox sitting quietly in their dugout, gloom and doom on their faces, and in our dugout, there was excitement and anticipation of what was to come. But there also was cautious optimism on our bench because we had seen what happened just two nights earlier.

But we had something the Red Sox did not. We had Jesse Orosco. He got pinch-hitter Ed Romero on a foul pop to Hernandez for the first out, and Wade Boggs on a bouncer to second baseman Wally Backman for the second. Only Marty Barrett stood in the way of our world championship.

The count went to 2–2 and I called for a fastball. Orosco threw a beauty. Barrett took a mighty swing… and missed…and the nicest sound I ever heard was the thud of the ball hitting my mitt. The greatest feeling was catching that third out. I jumped up from my crouch and started running toward the mound.

We were world champions! Orosco fired his glove into the air and then dropped to his knees with his arms held high as players poured out of the dugout and onto the field. Everybody engulfed Jesse on the mound in exultation.

The National League Championship Series ended with Orosco on the mound after striking out Kevin Bass, the final Astros batter, and the World Series ended with Orosco on the mound after striking out Marty Barrett, the final Red Sox batter. I had caught both final pitches. I gave Jesse the ball from the last pitch of the NLCS. The ball from the last pitch of the 1986 World Series was mine. I still have it—it is one of my prized possessions.

To a Major League Baseball player, there is no greater thrill than playing on a team that wins the World Series.

We were on top of the world!

6

Disappointment

THERE'S ONE BIG PROBLEM WHEN YOU REACH THE TOP of the world—when you fall, the descent will make your head spin.

After our dream season in 1986, when we won 108 games, finished 21½ games ahead of our nearest competitor, and won a world championship, we fell off to 92 wins in 1987 and finished in second place, three games behind the Cardinals.

Most teams would consider 92 wins and a second-place finish a successful season. We considered it a failure. Something was missing. We seemed to lack the fire and drive we had shown the previous season. At times we played as if we were simply going through the motions.

Maybe it's common for a team to have a letdown after such a dream season and winning a World Series, but it was more than that. We had problems on and off the field. We didn't seem to have the same camaraderie, spirit, and togetherness in the clubhouse that we had in 1986.

It started in spring training when we reported to camp without one of our leaders. Ray Knight had become a free

There's one big problem when you reach the top of the world—when you fall, the descent will make your head spin.

agent after the '86 season. He wanted to sign with the Mets, but they refused to meet his contract demands. We lost not only a good and productive third baseman but also a guy whose veteran experience, leadership, and wisdom were an invaluable part of our team.

Another guy that was missing was Kevin Mitchell, who was traded in the off season to the San Diego Padres for Kevin McReynolds. Mitchell would later be traded again to the San Francisco Giants, where he became National League MVP during the '84 season and the Giants won the World Series.

Then on April 1, 1987, Frank Cashen addressed us in a clubhouse meeting and told us that Doc Gooden had tested positive for cocaine and would be suspended and enter a drug rehabilitation program. Doc would miss the first two months of the season, and he wouldn't win his first game until June 5. When he returned, he pitched well and won 15 games. But in his first three years, he had averaged 19 wins a season. If he had won that many for us in 1987, it would have put us over the top.

Darryl Strawberry was another story. He was having marital problems and he often took his frustration out in the clubhouse. He seemed to change overnight from a guy who was outgoing and affable to one who was moody and hostile. A few years later, Darryl admitted he had a drinking problem, and he, too, entered rehab.

Around midseason, Strawberry started grumbling that he should be batting cleanup, my spot in the batting order. A couple of weeks later, when I looked at the lineup, Straw was in the number-four spot, and I had been dropped to sixth. It was obvious that Davey Johnson made the switch to appease Strawberry in an effort to motivate him and get him going. We needed Darryl's bat very badly.

I was disappointed when the move was made, but I never said anything to Davey. I wouldn't have been able to make a good case in any event. I was not having one of my better years. Not that I had a bad year—I batted .235 with 20 homers and 83 RBIs—but my numbers were not as good as they had been in '86. As it turned out, the move to the cleanup spot worked for Strawberry, who had his best season with a .284 average, 39 homers, 104 RBIs, and 36 stolen bases.

After the season, I started almost immediately on my training regiment to prepare myself for the 1988 season, when I would be playing at the age of 34 and in the next-to-last year of my seven-year contract. I was determined to have a good season and regain my cleanup spot in the batting order.

I never did get my cleanup spot back, although I had one of the best Aprils of my career with a .333 batting average, seven home runs, and 15 RBIs. On May 16, I hit the 299th home run of my career, and the New York newspapers began the "Carter Watch" for number 300. But my knees were killing me and I couldn't get the proper leverage in my swing, and the home run just would not come.

I went 78 games without a home run when finally, on August 11, I hit number 300 against the Cubs in Wrigley Field leading off the second inning against Al Nipper (yes, my old buddy with the Red Sox).

I played the entire second half of the season with aching knees, which took their toll on my hitting. After my fast start, I cooled off and finished with a batting average of .242, 11 homers (only four after April), and 46 RBIs. I was beginning to hear and read reports that I was washed up.

My only consolation was that the Mets had rebounded after our 1987 letdown and won the National League East by 15 games over the Pirates. To get to the World Series for the second time in three years, we had to win four out of seven games in the National League Championship Series against the Los Angeles Dodgers, a team we had beaten 11 times in 12 meetings during the regular season. There wasn't anybody, including those in our clubhouse, who thought we could lose to the Dodgers; another lesson that you can never take anything for granted in baseball, especially in a short series.

Game 1 in Dodger Stadium was another great pitching matchup: Doc Gooden, who had bounced back from his suspension and returned to his earlier greatness with 18 wins, against Orel Hershiser, who had a sensational season. Hershiser won 23 games, had an earned-run average of 2.26, pitched eight shutouts, and would be voted winner of the National League Cy Young Award.

The Dodgers touched Gooden up for a run in the first inning on a single and stolen base by Steve Sax and Mike

Marshall's RBI single. After that, Doc settled in and didn't allow another hit until the seventh, when Mike Scioscia doubled and Alfredo Griffin singled him home to make it 2–0.

As good as Doc was, Hershiser was even better. He blanked us through the first eight innings. If we were going to win this opening game, we were going to have to have another of those late-inning, come-from-behind rallies.

No problem! A rookie got us started. Gregg Jefferies singled to start the inning and moved to second on a ground-out by Keith Hernandez. Strawberry then drilled a double to center for one run that knocked Hershiser out of the game. The Dodgers called on their closer, Jay Howell, and he walked Kevin McReynolds. Howard Johnson struck out for the second out of the inning and wouldn't you know it, it was my turn to bat with the tying and go-ahead runs on base and two outs. How often I had found myself in a position like that.

Howell got ahead of me with two curveballs for strikes, and then he tried to get me to chase another curveball down and away, out of the strike zone. It might have been a ball, but it was too close to take. The last thing I wanted to do was have the game end with my bat on my shoulder, so I reached for it and hit one of those dying quails to center field.

The Dodgers were in a "no doubles" defense and center fielder John Shelby was playing me almost with his back to the fence. He had a long run for the ball. He made a valiant effort, dove for the ball, and just missed it by inches. Strawberry scored from second, and McReynolds, off with the crack of the bat, came tearing around third. He charged home and bowled over catcher Mike Scioscia to score what turned out to be the winning run when Randy Myers retired the Dodgers in order in the bottom of the ninth.

We were feeling pretty good about ourselves, winning Game 1 in Los Angeles, taking the home-field advantage away from the Dodgers, and with David Cone set to pitch Game 2. Coney had had a phenomenal year, with a record of 20–3 and an earned-run average of 2.22. He would finish second to Hershiser in the voting for the National League Cy Young Award. We couldn't help thinking *sweep.*

> *We couldn't help thinking sweep.*

Cone is an upbeat, outgoing guy, a favorite of writers. He was always accessible and quotable, and a little outspoken. The *New York Daily News* had hired Coney to write a column covering the series, and David didn't pull any punches in his piece that ran the day after the first game. He took shots at both Hershiser and Howell, especially Howell. Cone said Howell's curveball reminded him of a Little League pitcher.

It's no surprise that Dodgers manager Tommy Lasorda, a master psychologist, got hold of the column and plastered it all over his clubhouse, highlighting the negative passages as a means of motivating the Dodgers for Game 2. Cone later apologized for his remarks, but it was too late. Lasorda's psychology worked, as the Dodgers scored a run off Cone in the first and then pounded him out of the game with a four-run second. The series was tied, one game each. There would be no sweep. Still, we felt good with a split in L.A., going home to Shea Stadium for the next three games.

In Game 3, the Dodgers jumped out to an early 3–0 lead, but again we battled back, scoring a run in the bottom of the third and two in the sixth, and putting the game away with a five-run eighth.

The series turned in Game 4, or to be more accurate, with one pitch in Game 4. Gooden started and just as he had done in Game 1, he was touched up in the first inning, this time for two runs. Here we go again, forced to come from behind. We took the lead in the fourth on homers by Strawberry and McReynolds. In the sixth, McReynolds doubled, and I hit a triple to make it 4–2.

Again, as he had done in Game 1, Doc settled down and pitched great, holding the Dodgers to one hit after the first and striking out nine as he took the 4–2 lead into the ninth inning. He started the ninth by walking Shelby, always a bad sign, especially with a two-run lead. Shelby can't hurt you. Let him hit his way on. It meant the Dodgers would bring the tying run to the plate.

Mike Scioscia was the batter, and he hit Gooden's first pitch over the wall in right field. The game was tied. Suddenly, a strange silence came over Shea Stadium. The crowd was stunned. So were we. Scioscia had hit only three home runs all season, and here he had hit what would be the biggest home run in his career. We were forced to play another extra-inning game.

Were we deflated by Scioscia's home run? Possibly. Certainly, the home run was the turning point in the series. We didn't score again and the Dodgers won the game, 5–4, on Kirk Gibson's home run off of Roger McDowell in the top of the twelfth. The series was tied at two games apiece.

It was a different Dodgers team that came out for Game 5, energized and more confident after Scioscia's and Gibson's home runs. They beat us 7–4 and took a three-games-to-two lead in the series. We were faced with having to go to Los Angeles and win two games in Dodger Stadium.

David Cone gave us a lift and atoned for his poor start in Game 2 by winning Game 6, 5–1, with a five-hitter. But in Game 7, the Dodgers struck early, a run in the first and a big five in the second. With Hershiser pitching at his best, we had no chance for a comeback this time. Orel held us to just five hits and the Dodgers finished us off, 6–0.

> *We won one World Series in my five years with the Mets, but I will always believe we were better than that.*

Losing that series to the Dodgers was the biggest disappointment of my playing career. We won one World Series in my five years with the Mets, but I will always believe we were better than that. We should have won at least one more, maybe two.

Would I ever again experience the joy of playing for a world championship team? Time was running out.

7

Coming Full Circle

AS THE 1989 SEASON APPROACHED, I FOUND MYSELF AT another career crossroads, entering the last year of my seven-year contract. When the season ended, I would be a free agent, so it was imperative that I have a good year in order to get a contract extension from the Mets or, if not, gain my freedom and make myself available to the highest bidder. I could see one more long-term, lucrative contract in my immediate future, just one more before I retired from the game as a player.

I kind of thought the Mets might extend my contract after the 1986 season, when we won the World Series and I hit 24 homers, knocked in 105 runs, and finished third in the Most Valuable Player voting. Or after the 1988 season, when we won our division and I was one year away from free agency. But they didn't.

Even though my body was barking at me—my right knee and right elbow had started acting up again at the end of the 1988 season—I truly felt I still had at least three or four good years left.

I wouldn't reach my 35th birthday until the first week of the '89 season, and while 35 may be old for a catcher, I had been playing the position for only 16 years. Because I never caught until I signed a professional contract, I had staved off years of the wear and tear that comes with squatting behind the plate and colliding with runners at home, abuse you incur as a catcher at any level.

In the winter between the '88 and '89 seasons, I paid a visit to the famed sports orthopedist Dr. James Andrews in Birmingham, Alabama. He gave me a complete checkup and pronounced me good to go for the upcoming season. I was further encouraged when I arrived in spring training when manager Davey Johnson came up to me and said, "I'm going to name you cocaptain."

I had felt slighted the year before when Keith Hernandez was named captain, and I told Davey so. He obviously thought it over and agreed that I should share the honor with Keith. The way I figured it, the manager isn't going to make me cocaptain without the knowledge and approval of the front office, and the Mets are not going to give a guy the title if they have no intention of re-signing him.

My good feeling was shattered a few weeks later when my knee blew up again and swelled to twice its normal size. Doctors drained fluid from the knee, shot it full of cortisone, and said I was fine. I knew better and should have said so. Instead, I played through the pain. For the $2 million they were paying me, the Mets didn't want me on the sideline. By May, they had no choice. Again my knee swelled and had to be drained of fluid and shot with cortisone, and I landed on the disabled list.

At the time, I had been to bat only 79 times and was hitting a paltry .114.

After spending 15 days on the disabled list, I tried to come back by catching batting practice while the team was in San Diego. If I passed the test, I would be activated and get back in the lineup. But the next day the knee blew up again, so I paid a visit to Dr. Ralph Gambardella in the office of noted orthopedist Dr. Frank Jobe. Dr. Gambardella recommended surgery, so I immediately flew to Birmingham to see Dr. Andrews.

On May 29, coincidentally the same day Mike Schmidt announced his retirement from baseball, Dr. Andrews operated on my knee to remove eight loose bodies and two synovial cysts. The surgery sidelined me for almost two months.

At the end of July, I went to the Mets' Triple A Tidewater farm team in the International League on a rehab assignment. After five games, the Mets brought me back at the urging of manager Davey Johnson, who wanted me for the August and September stretch in the pennant chase. I shouldn't have gone. I wasn't ready to play, but the Mets were in a pennant race and they needed me. And I was in the last year of my contract, so I wanted to prove that I could still play.

I managed to raise my batting average to a still-dismal .183. I played in only 50 games and had two home runs

I shouldn't have gone. I wasn't ready to play, but the Mets were in a pennant race and they needed me. And I was in the last year of my contract, so I wanted to prove that I could still play.

and 15 RBIs. The knee injury cost me a chance to tie a record held by Bill Dickey and Johnny Bench of catching at least 100 games in each of 13 consecutive seasons. My streak ended at 12 seasons in 1989.

We finished in second place, six games behind the Cubs, and the Mets made a decision. On October 3, they announced that Keith Hernandez and I, cocaptains, would not be re-signed.

I later found out from Davey Johnson that the Mets had actually made their decision months earlier. Davey said, "I was told not to play you."

I thought back and remembered that in one of my first games back after surgery, on August 9 in Philadelphia, I had four hits. The next day, we returned home for a doubleheader against the Cardinals, and I didn't start in either game. I pinch hit in both games and got a single in the first game and a sacrifice fly in the second.

I did start two days later and doubled in my first at-bat, giving me six consecutive hits. I also singled in my last at-bat of that game. But I realized later that the Mets didn't want me to do well because they had made up their minds

It was a case of "What have you done for us lately?"

they were not going to re-sign me. Yet they had rushed me back, urged me to play, and, like a fool, I did it. So much for loyalty, which I found out was a one-way street. But that is the nature of the business.

The Mets used me and discarded me, even though they had no catcher coming along to replace me (Todd Hundley would not arrive until the following season). It was a case of "What have you done for us lately?"

Although technically I wasn't considered a free agent, I still had the right to sign with any team, which should have been a reason for joy, a chance for a bonanza on the open market. But what bargaining power did I have as a 35-year-old, oft-injured catcher who had batted .183 with two homers and 15 RBIs in 153 at-bats in his free-agent year?

• • •

For the first time, I found doors closing to me. The Atlanta Braves were the first team to contact me. Bobby Cox was the general manager at the time and he wanted me to join them. He said, "We can offer you $500,000."

I thought, "Hey, I just made over $2 million." Just two years before, I was the highest-paid player in baseball. I would have had to take a 75 percent cut in pay.

At the time, the Braves were a bad team—more precisely, a young team beginning to rebuild. They had finished last in the National League West in 1989. At that stage of my career, I didn't want to go to a last-place team. I wanted to go to a veteran team with a chance to win.

In retrospect, I probably should have taken the Braves' offer. Cox took over as manager that year, and the next year he began a run in which he led the Braves to 14 division titles in 15 years. If I had gone with them and worked with guys like Tom Glavine, Greg Maddux, and John Smoltz, that would have been a good way to end my career. I might have been credited with helping to bring along that young pitching staff and starting the Braves on their incredible run of division championships. Who knows, I might even have wound up being a coach under Cox, and that might have led to getting a major league managing job.

That's hindsight, however, and I try never to look back. As it turned out, I got a call from Al Rosen, general manager of the Giants, who made me an offer that, with incentives, would pay me double what the Braves were offering.

The Giants had just been in the World Series the year before, and I was hoping to be a part of another World Series team. The Giants wanted a veteran catcher to handle a veteran pitching staff. They had Rick Reuschel, Atlee Hammaker, Mike LaCoss, Steve Bedrosian, Kelly Downs, and Scott Garrelts—all older guys.

For the first time in 15 years I was not a regular player. I was a platoon player, sharing the catching duties with Terry Kennedy, but it was a fun year, one of my most enjoyable seasons. I loved playing for manager Roger Craig. I had a pretty good year, nine homers and 27 RBIs in 244 at-bats, and I think I proved to people that I could still play.

After the season, I became an unrestricted free agent again. One night while I was asleep, the phone rang, and when I answered it I heard a familiar voice bellowing into the phone, "Gary, this is Tommy Lasorda of the Los Angeles Dodgers. I'd really like you to come and play for our team. But all we can offer you is to come to camp as an on-roster invitee and compete for a job."

With no other takers, I had no choice, so I agreed to go. I was excited because I was going back home to Southern California, to play for the team I had rooted for as a kid.

I went to the Dodgers' spring-training camp in Vero Beach and had a pretty good spring. I thought things were looking good. The Dodgers had given me uniform No. 12. For the first time since my first two spring trainings with the Expos, I had a jersey other than No. 8. Joey Amalfitano, the longtime Dodgers third-base coach, had No. 8. When I felt I had a good chance to make the team, I went to Joey and told him I'd really like to wear No. 8. "If I make the club," I said, "is there a chance I could wear No. 8?"

I later learned that when Juan Samuel went to the Dodgers, he also wanted No. 8 and Joey turned him down. This time he told me, "If you make the club, you've got it."

Sure enough, I made the club and Joey gave me the number.

In some ways it was a disappointing season. Lasorda had promised me I was going to play a lot, and that's all I wanted to do. As of May 7, 1991, five weeks into the season, I had only 15 at-bats. I started one game against the Braves and threw out three base runners, including Deion Sanders.

I called Sandy, and I said, "Honey, I don't know if this is working out."

I was closing in on 2,000 hits and 1,000 runs scored, nice milestones to have before my career ended. I knew my career was winding down. I had just passed my 37th birthday, and it was about that time that I thought of my mom, who had died at the age of 37 and whose grave was not far from Dodger Stadium. I knew the end of my career was near, and I was contemplating leaving the game.

Sandy said, "Don't give up, honey. God has opened this door for a purpose. Just hang in there, your opportunity will come. Stick it out and see what you can do. Maybe you'll get your chance."

It turned out that about a week later, Mike Scioscia, the regular catcher, took a foul tip and broke his hand. He went on the disabled list, and I played every game for two straight weeks, including both games of a double-header against the Braves. Knowing I was going to be in the lineup every day, I started hitting and playing well. It wasn't the flip of the coin, every now and then, as it had been when Scioscia was there.

> *Knowing I was going to be in the lineup every day, I started hitting and playing well.*

I helped the Dodgers get into first place. By the All-Star break, we had a five-game lead over the Reds and a nine-and-a-half-game lead over the Braves.

When Scioscia came back I was given more of an opportunity to play, but Scioscia got his starting job back and played most of the time, even against left-handers. I was frustrated because I just wanted to play. Throughout my career I always knew in advance when I was going to play or be given a rest. With the Dodgers I would have to go to Bill Russell, the bench coach, and say, "Ropes, is there a chance I'm going to play tomorrow? There's a left-hander going."

Russell would say, "I don't know. I've got some good vibes."

Good vibes? What did that mean? I just wanted to know if I was playing.

We wound up getting beat out of the division by the Braves by one game. We played our final game against the Giants in Candlestick Park in San Francisco. I didn't start, but I got in as a pinch-hitter and grounded to shortstop. I really believed that was going to be the last game I ever played, and I got very emotional. I remember telling my teammate, Stan Javier, "I think that might have been my last game."

After the season, the Dodgers put me on waivers and to my surprise, the Expos claimed me and brought me back to Montreal, where I had played the first 10 years of my career and where I always felt the love of the fans. I figured this would be a great way to end my career.

It was the intention of the Expos, who were not drawing well, to bring me back to help put people in the seats but not really play me. That didn't sit well with me, and when I talked with general manager Dan Duquette and president Bill Stoneman to negotiate a contract, I said, "I think I can still play, and I want to come back to finish my career and play, not just to sit and put fannies in the seats."

It was the intention of the Expos, who were not drawing well, to bring me back to help put people in the seats but not really play me.

The Expos were not a good team in 1991, the year before I got there. They won only 71 games and finished in last place in the National League East, 26½ games out of first. But in 1992, with good young players like Moises Alou, Delino DeShields, Marquis Grissom, and Larry Walker; 16-game winners Ken Hill and Dennis Martinez; and an outstanding closer in John Wetteland, who saved 37 games, the improvement was amazing. We won 87 games and finished in second place.

The Expos had a young player named Darrin Fletcher and he was being groomed to be their regular catcher. I was there to back him up and kind of help groom him for the job. Fletcher got sick during the season, which led to a collapsed lung, and he had to go on the disabled list, giving me the opportunity to start playing on a regular basis. I like to think I was at least partly responsible for helping the Expos improve. I played in 95 games and did pretty well. I went over the 2,000 mark in games caught and over the 1,200 mark in RBIs, the last little milestones I wanted to reach.

I'm proud to say I'm one of four catchers to have scored more than 1,000 runs and had more than 2,000 hits, more than 300 home runs, and more than 1,200 runs batted in. The others are Yogi Berra, Johnny Bench, and Carlton Fisk, and that's pretty good company to be in.

Near the middle of September, I came to realize that my body was broken down and the time had come to announce my retirement. When I made my decision, I felt relieved, but at the press conference, I broke down emotionally. I was in my 18th full season at 38 years of age and it was tough to let the game go.

I might have been able to play another year or two, but as I look back I'm glad I didn't. My last game that I was going to play in was planned. Felipe Alou wanted me to play the last game of the homestand, and he was going to bat me cleanup. The game was a week after I had announced my retirement. The way I finished was perfect, in front of a fan-appreciation crowd of almost 42,000 people in Montreal.

They say you're only as good as your last at-bat. Well, mine was a game-winning double in the seventh inning that drove in the only run in a 1–0 victory in front of a big crowd, and I left the field to a standing ovation when I was taken out for a pinch runner.

I couldn't have scripted a better way to finish my playing career. I started my major league career as a Montreal Expo, and I ended it as a Montreal Expo. It was a storybook ending.

8

My Life, Part II

IT WAS OVER, AND I KNEW IT!

Nobody had to tell me. I felt it in my body: the aching elbow, the cranky knees, the broken thumbs. I could read it in my statistics for that 1992 season: 95 games for the Montreal Expos, five home runs, 29 runs batted in, an average of .218, some 44 points below my lifetime average for 19 major league seasons if you want to include nine games with the Expos in 1974. I saw it in my birth certificate: 38 my last birthday, more than halfway to age 39.

All of a sudden, I was faced with a decision. What to do with the rest of my life?

Most people at age 38 are into their careers and in their prime years, but here I was finished with one career, too young, too energetic, and too ambitious to retire but kind of old to be starting out in something new.

All of a sudden, I was faced with a decision. What to do with the rest of my life?

It wasn't that I needed the money. I had made enough money playing baseball, more than most people make their entire lives, and I had provided for my family with annuities and trust funds for my three children. I had planned for my golden years with a portfolio set up by my financial adviser, who started out with me when I played in Montreal and who has been with me for more than 20 years.

But I needed something to do.

For more than 30 years of my life, all the way back to Little League, I had done something I thoroughly enjoyed, playing baseball, and now it was time to turn the page. That chapter had come to an end, and there was an emptiness in my life. I was suddenly forced to face reality and to answer the question, what am I going to do with the rest of my life?

My mom was only 37 when she passed away, and here I was the same age and faced with the indecisiveness of my future.

It had really hit home for me one day in Dodger Stadium the previous year, 1991, when I was playing for the Los Angeles Dodgers. At the time, we were living close to Loma Vista Cemetery in Fullerton, where my mother was buried. My mom was only 37 when she passed away, and here I was the same age and faced with the indecisiveness of my future. Thoughts like that have a way of putting you in touch with your own mortality.

I was just beginning the second phase of my life with no plans and no real prospects. I wasn't trained for anything other than baseball. Provided I stayed healthy, I had all these productive years ahead of me, and I wanted to make the most of them.

All professional athletes are faced with the same dilemma when they retire. There must be a high percentage of players who made a lot of money but when they got out of the game they didn't know what to do with themselves, and before they knew it, they were bankrupt. Granted, with today's salaries, the upper-echelon players don't have too many financial worries, but all athletes once they retire, no matter how financially secure they may be, face the problem of withdrawal and how to spend their remaining years productively.

Three weeks after I retired, I had an interview with the Florida Marlins, and I was hired as a television color commentator on Marlins games.

I thought broadcasting was going to be my thing. I did that for four years, and I truly believed I was making progress in television. I felt I was developing my own style. Some fans liked my style, but others were critical, and that surprised me. I know you're never going to please everybody, but I thought, "What do they want?" I was just trying to be me, trying to be real, trying to teach fans the game by passing along insights I had acquired in my 19 years of playing the game. I thought I had a great deal to contribute, especially in the Miami area, where they had an expansion team and many fans were new to Major League Baseball.

The Marlins asked me to return for a fifth year to do pregame and postgame analysis, but I declined because I learned there was an opening in Montreal. I had preliminary talks with the Expos to be a color commentator on their games. It was only a 25-game schedule compared to

115 games with the Marlins, which suited me fine. Not only would I be reassociated with the team I had played with for 11 years and get a chance to work with a true broadcasting legend, Dave Van Horne, but also the lighter schedule would allow me to spend more time coaching my daughter Kimmy's high school softball team at Kings Academy.

I was offered the Expos job, and I accepted it. I liked working with Van Horne and learned a great deal from him, but it was somewhat frustrating because we did so few games. We'd do two or three games and then we might go four weeks before we did another game. I don't think there was one time that we ever did as many as four games in a row. What I thought would be a benefit was turning out to be a problem for me. I tried my best to keep up with developments with the team through the newspapers or on television, but there's no substitute for being there day after day. If you're not around the team on a daily basis, there is no continuity; you lose touch with what's going on with the team.

I broadcast Expos games for three years, and then, in 2000, the Expos lost their radio and television contracts. By that time I had been broadcasting for seven years and I had come to realize it wasn't my passion. I was itching to get back into uniform. I missed the competition and the routine. But I was 45 years old, and I had been out of uniform for seven years. All of a sudden I was at the crossroads once more with no job and no prospects.

I decided to try golf. I was a pretty good golfer, so I worked at sharpening my game, and I joined the celebrity golf tour. I had lowered my handicap to a three and was doing fairly well on the tour when, in January 2001, the Mets asked me if I would be interested in coaching in their organization. I said I absolutely would be interested because that's where my heart was. The Mets wanted me to be a roving catching instructor, which was perfect. I found I could work for the Mets, still continue to play on the celebrity golf tour, and spend time with the family.

My job as a roving instructor, which consisted of traveling through the Mets' minor league system and visiting every affiliate at every minor league level to work with the catchers, was only part time, and the Mets allowed me to make my own schedule. I spent the entire six weeks in spring training, which I enjoyed a great deal and which came before the celebrity tour got started. During the season, the Mets gave me the flexibility of choosing my own schedule, so I was able to go to their minor league affiliates to work with the catchers and still play most tournaments on the celebrity tour.

Once I was back in uniform, visible and back "in the mix," so to speak, I figured it was just a matter of the right opportunity coming along at the right time for me to start on a path toward one day becoming a big-league manager. Perhaps if I had started on that road immediately after my playing days were over, I might have become a major league manager by now. I'll

Perhaps if I had started on that road immediately after my playing days were over, I might have become a major league manager by now. I'll never know.

never know. I had a choice to make back then, and I don't regret the choice I made.

When I retired from playing, my children were 14, 12, and eight years old, and I had already missed so much of their formative years. I wasn't going to let that happen again. The broadcasting job in Florida meant some traveling, but for home games, I was able to live in my own home, only an hour's drive from Joe Robbie Stadium. That allowed me to attend many of my children's functions. Working in Florida also afforded me the opportunity to coach my daughter Kimmy's high school softball team. In her senior year, Kimmy was named Player of the Year in AA, and she was awarded a scholarship to Florida State.

When the position with the Mets came along, my kids were close to being on their own or in college, so I was free to get started on working toward becoming a major league manager.

Being back in the game, in uniform, working with young players, I caught the attention of other teams, as I thought I might. In September 2002, I thought I had become a Yankee. Well, not a Yankee exactly, but the manager of their Triple A team, Columbus, in the International League.

My old Mets teammate Doc Gooden was working for the Yankees at the time, and when he learned that they were looking for a manager for Columbus, Doc mentioned me to Billy Connors, a longtime employee of the Yankees whom I knew when he was pitching coach for the Chicago Cubs. One thing led to another and I got a phone call from Mark Newman, vice president of baseball operations for the Yankees. We talked about my managing the Columbus Clippers and I thought I had the job.

In fact, I was so sure I had the job and so excited, I told everybody about it. I called friends, family members, and pastors. I called my dad and said, "You're talking to the next manager of the Columbus Clippers."

In November, Newman called me and said he was sorry, but the Yankees had decided to go in another direction. I was disappointed because I thought it had been a done deal. When they gave the job to Bucky Dent it was clear that they had decided to go with someone who had been in their organization, and I understood that.

When the Columbus job fell through, I continued working as a roving catching instructor for the Mets, which suited me fine. I wound up doing that for four years and enjoyed it immensely. I liked teaching, and I especially liked working with young players. But after four years, I was ready for a new challenge.

9

Managing in the Minors

IN 2005, 13 YEARS AFTER I RETIRED AS AN ACTIVE PLAYER, I found what I believe is my true future calling.

The timing was right. Our older daughter, Christy, had been married three years earlier. Our younger daughter, Kimmy, was planning to get married that year. And our son, D.J., our youngest, was a junior at Samford University in Birmingham, Alabama. With our children pretty much on their own, I told Sandy that now was the time for me to embark on a managing career. As usual, Sandy was completely supportive. She encouraged me to go for it.

I expressed my interest in managing to the Mets, but I emphasized that I didn't want something handed to me because of who I am. I suggested they start me in the lowest rookie league, and they did; they named me manager of Port St. Lucie, their entry-level team in the Gulf Coast Rookie League. Ironically, it's the same league where I had started my professional playing career 33 years earlier.

As soon as I put on that uniform, I learned something about myself. I loved managing. I loved working with kids. I loved being in uniform. That's where my heart

> *As soon as I put on that uniform, I learned something about myself. I loved managing. I loved working with kids. I loved being in uniform. That's where my heart is.*

is. That's where I belong. Once I got the feel for what it was like to be a full-time manager—the bus trips, the long hours, the attention to detail, and the demands on my time—I loved it, every minute of it. I made up my mind that some day I was going to be a major league manager. I thought then and I still think I could be a good one.

Having been a minor league manager, I think I now know what it takes to be a good big-league manager, but do I really know? I've never done it, and until I have, I really can't know. I know a lot of responsibility is put on a big-league manager that minor league managers don't have to face. It takes working with the media, being fan friendly, and caring for your players. I have the greatest appreciation and respect for those who have done it and have been successful. I think I can be successful, too. I believe my qualifications are there. I'm confident I can handle it, but I won't know until I've done it. I would love the opportunity to try. I accept the fact that it might not happen. If it does, it would be a blessing.

• • •

When the Mets asked me to be a roving catching instructor back in 2001, my eyes lit up like a Christmas tree because I had been wanting to get back in uniform. I enjoyed doing that, going first to the big-league camp in spring training and then to the minor league camp. I was excited because I was part of it again. That's where my heart is.

The one drawback with being a rover is that you go from one minor league affiliate to another. You're in one place for three or four days, and then you leave and won't see those guys for another month, so you lose touch. After four years of being a rover, I started managing, and that really excited me. I was so pumped up about it. You get an identity with a team. You can accomplish so much more when you spend the entire season with the same kids, helping them improve, watching them grow, and following their progress. It's such a treat to work with kids right out of high school or college when they are so eager to learn.

> *You get an identity with a team. You can accomplish so much more when you spend the entire season with the same kids, helping them improve, watching them grow, and following their progress.*

As a broadcaster, I often felt alienated. I'd walk into the clubhouse or hang around the cage during batting practice in Florida and Montreal and, except for a few veterans, players would turn their backs on me. They viewed me as part of the media or an arm of management and treated me like an adversary. I missed being in uniform, and I missed the competition and camaraderie.

When you're a manager, at any level, winning and losing becomes important. I loved the preparation for a game. A minor league manager doesn't have a full complement of coaches, so I found myself doing a little of everything, including pitching batting practice, and coaching on the lines at third base. As the third-base coach, I was playing the game while I was coaching. I was into it. I was focused. Situations would arise, and I found myself thinking like a player.

Managing in the minor leagues means spending 10 to 12 hours a day, every day, at the ballpark, pitching batting practice; hitting fungoes; coaching at third base; dealing with the media (what little of it there is in the minors); being hitting, fielding, and base-running instructor; taking on the role of counselor, father confessor, and surrogate parent to your players; and, when the game is over, doing the laborious, tedious, time-consuming job of filing reports on every player, after every game, with the front office. And you do all of it for very little money. So little money, in fact, that very few former major league players who earned seven figures playing the game are willing to go to the minor leagues to manage. In fact, some former big-league stars have refused to manage in the minor leagues because they considered it demeaning, and others, for whom the game came so easy, lacked the patience to put up with the failures of players less talented than they were.

I was willing to go to the minor leagues. I have the patience. Because I wanted to learn how to manage, I was willing to work for less money than I made as a player, but having spent four years as a rover, I had already built up my salary so that I was earning more than the average minor league manager. For that I thank the Mets for their generosity.

I loved everything about managing, every little detail, and was willing to continue to learn with the ultimate goal of becoming a big-league manager some day.

Part of managing in the minors was working in concert with the front office and understanding that process when it comes to dealing with prospects. For example, I was given five priority players and was told they had to bat one through five in the lineup, regardless of how they were doing.

I felt it was my responsibility as a manager to meet the requirements of the front office and still impart to my players the incentive to learn and improve, and to give them constructive criticism when necessary. I was no different from most managers in that I had two basic rules that I asked my players to observe: play hard and show up on time.

I loved everything about managing, every minute detail, and was willing to continue to learn with the ultimate goal of becoming a big-league manager some day.

My style was to talk to each one of my players individually. I'd call them into my office one at a time and tell them I promised to do everything I could to give them every opportunity to prove themselves. I explained that there were priority players who I was told I had to play every day. I told them, "If you're in the lineup and you prove to me that you really want this by hustling and playing hard every day, that will merit an opportunity to play the next day."

These kids played their butts off. It was because I was on a one-on-one basis with them. If a kid was struggling,

I'd sit him down and give somebody else who was not a priority player a chance to play.

Part of player development, to me, is to teach kids how to play the game and to teach them how to win and have that follow them right up the ladder. If they don't know how to win when they get to the big leagues, they're going to be complacent and they're not going to have that hunger to win.

In my first year as a manager, we had the best record in the Gulf Coast League, but we lost to the Yankees affiliate in the playoffs. Managing was a treat. I was working with kids just out of high school or college. It was a rewarding season, and I loved it.

The next year, the Mets wanted me to go to Binghamton to manage their team in the class AA Eastern League, but I asked them if I had a choice, why not let me stay in Port St. Lucie and manage their team in the class A Florida State League. Even though it was a lower classification than Binghamton, at least it would keep me close to home. The Mets agreed, and we won the 2006 Florida State League championship.

Sandy and I went to the ring ceremony and many of those kids came up to me and were so excited, they gave me a hug. That was very rewarding for me. Those kids were so proud of those rings. I told them they might get a ring only once in their whole career, so they should cherish it. I played in one World Series, and, believe me, the World Series ring means more than anyone can ever know.

When the season was over and the Mets were making their plans for 2007, I got a call from Tony Bernazard, who is the right-hand man for Mets general manager Omar Minaya. Tony said they wanted me to go to Binghamton. He said, "This is where we want you to be." I still wanted to be close to my family, so I said, "Tony, if I still have to be in the minor leagues, why not let me just stay in Port St. Lucie? What's the difference? I'm managing and it's still in the organization and if you talk about player development, I'd still be able to do that with the kids."

"No," Tony said. "That's not going to happen."

Then I said, "Let me go to New Orleans [the Mets' Triple A farm team in the Pacific Coast League] and be the hitting instructor [after Howard was named the first base coach]."

No to that. No to going back to Port St. Lucie. No to going back as a roving instructor. No to everything.

At the same time, my name came up for a few other jobs. The Mets' first-base coaching position was open and my name was being mentioned along with Ken Oberkfell, the Mets' Triple A manager, and Howard Johnson, a former Mets third baseman who had been in their organization for several years as a minor league coach. Johnson was chosen, and I was glad for him because he had paid his dues. He had been in the organization for several years and moved up the ladder. He deserved the chance to be a big-league coach.

I also heard from the Dodgers and interviewed for the job as manager of their Triple A farm team in Las Vegas and didn't get that.

I interviewed for the Colorado Rockies' hitting coach job and didn't get that.

And the Mets were being adamant. I had one option with them: go to Binghamton to manage. I chose not to go.

Am I disappointed? Absolutely! I felt I did what the Mets wanted me to do and that was to get managerial experience. I thought there would be a chance for me to move up the ladder and eventually get to the big leagues as a manager.

In retrospect maybe I should have gone to Binghamton because as this is written, I'm out of baseball.

Do I regret not going to Binghamton? In retrospect, maybe I should have gone to Binghamton because as this is written, I'm out of baseball.

Don't misunderstand. The Mets' organization, Fred and Jeff Wilpon and so many others, have been very good to me. They were wonderful when I was elected to the Hall of Fame in 2003, honoring me with a day at Shea Stadium, and I'll always be grateful. I spent five great years with the Mets, made many friends in New York, and, in my heart, I will continue to think of myself as a Met, especially since the Expos no longer exist. With the Expos gone, I feel disenfranchised. I don't have a team association except with the Mets. I thought I was going to be able to dedicate myself to the Mets organization.

• • •

Once I got a taste of managing, I knew that was what I wanted to do. As a former catcher, I believed I had an advantage.

Have you ever wondered why so many catchers become managers? When the 2007 season began, 10 of the 30 major league managers, 33 percent, had some playing experience as a catcher. Connie Mack, the granddaddy of all managers with 53 years on the job, was a catcher. Branch Rickey, considered by many to be the greatest baseball mind ever, was a catcher. So were Bill Carrigan, Yogi Berra, Mickey Cochrane, Gil Hodges, Darrell Johnson, Al Lopez, Jack McKeon, Gabby Street, Luke Sewell, Joe Torre, and Wilbert Robinson, all pennant-winning managers.

As a catcher, you have the whole game in front of you. You're like a second manager on the field. When I was catching, I used to look over to the dugout in certain situations, such as when we needed to walk a guy to set up a double play or a force at any base. By looking at the manager, it would be a hint that I thought we should walk the hitter. There were times in my playing career that just by looking I may have influenced a manager into making a move.

As a catcher, you have the whole game in front of you. You're like a second manager on the field.

When I was playing, I studied the game to the extent that I took pride in my pitching staff having the best earned-run average in the league almost every year. I watched TV and I checked the newspapers every day to see who was hot and who was not. For example, if we had the Pirates coming up on our schedule, I would check their box scores very closely to see who their hot hitters were. If Bill Madlock, a four-time batting champion, was swinging a hot bat, I was going to pitch him a little differently. He was one guy I wouldn't let beat us.

A catcher's perspective is different from any other player's. You have the alignment of your defense in front of you at all times, so I got into the habit of checking my defense with each batter to see if they were playing in the right position, or if they had to be moved. Because I became so used to doing that in my playing days, I carried that over into my managing.

Catchers also get to learn about handling pitchers; when they're losing it, when they're tired and so on, you have to know what to do to get them back on track. You carry that over into managing also. As a manager, the only thing I wanted to do from the bench was control the running game. I would call pitchouts, throwovers, and slide steps, all with the intention of controlling the opposition's running game. Except for that, I wanted my catchers to call their own game. That's the only way a catcher is going to earn the respect of his pitchers, and it's the only way he's going to learn. If the manager is calling the pitches, how is the catcher going to learn?

Friends have asked me, "Gary, why did you want to manage in the minor leagues with all the headaches?"

I told them why, and I'll tell you.

It was because of my love and passion for the game. As a player you get accustomed to a routine. When you stop playing you miss that routine, you miss the camaraderie with your teammates, and, most of all, you miss the game and the competition. You've been a part of it for so long, it's hard to let go.

Look at how many players, great players, retired and sat out a few years and swore they would never go back. They didn't like the traveling, and they didn't like the pressure and the daily grind. And then after a few years, they're aching to get back. Don Mattingly and Ron Guidry came back to be coaches; Ray Knight and Joe Girardi came back as managers, and when they lost those jobs, they came back again as broadcasters. So many others, like Keith Hernandez, Ron Darling, Rick Sutcliffe, Tony Gwynn, Joe Morgan, Mark Grace, and Eric Karros, who missed the game so much, also came back as broadcasters.

When you stop playing you miss that routine, you miss the camaraderie with your teammates, and, most of all, you miss the game and the competition.

I certainly can understand why they came back. You need to keep yourself motivated with something you love to do. You have to have a passion for something. A lot of players, when they retire from the game, get into businesses such as selling insurance or running a family company. Are they really happy? Most of them, because they had been in the game so long and because they miss it, want to get back into it.

A former player, because he's still a relatively young man, gets to the point where he wonders what he's going to do with the rest of his life. He's too young to be totally retired and do nothing. How much golf can you play? There are only so many fish you can catch. So he looks to get back into the game he loves so much, where he earned his identity.

That's probably going to change in the future because the modern player is making so much money. He's not going to want to go back to the game and make $35,000 as a minor league manager or $100,000 as a coach if he made $18 or $20 million as a player. I can't see Derek Jeter or Alex Rodriguez becoming a minor league manager or even a major league coach.

Players like that don't need to concern themselves with where their next dollars are going to be earned. In my case, it's a little bit different. Am I okay financially? Yes, for the most part. But with the lifestyle we've become accustomed to, I'm going to have to earn money to continue that lifestyle.

What is going to be my source of income? Certainly not being a minor league manager. I would like to maintain my lifestyle, but I also need something to motivate me each day. I don't want to wake up each morning and have nothing else to look forward to than hitting a golf ball. I want to get involved in an activity that is gratifying, one in which I can give something back.

> *I want to get involved in an activity that is gratifying, one in which I can give something back.*

That's why in 2000, I started the Gary Carter Foundation, which has raised $8 million to fight leukemia, the disease that took my mother from me. To diversify, the foundation also gives financial support to nine schools in underprivileged areas. The reason I got involved with schools is that both of our daughters became teachers. Christy, our oldest, taught third- and fourth-grade gifted children until she became a full-time mom. Kimmy taught English at the local independent middle school and was the softball coach. Later, she taught ninth-grade English and was the soccer coach at her high school alma mater. Today, she's head softball coach at Palm Beach Atlantic University.

Obviously, I didn't take a minor league managing job for the money. I can earn more money making appearances and speeches and at card shows. I took a minor league managing job because I love the game and because I believe I have something to offer. Baseball is where my passion is. I was willing to pay my dues. I was willing to continue managing in the low minor leagues for as long as it took. I was willing to do whatever I had to do because I love the game.

I strongly believe that a man is most happy when he's working and enjoying being in the workplace. When I retired from playing, I realized I needed to do something with the rest of my life. I tried broadcasting, I tried being a roving instructor, and then I found managing. I'm in my fifties, but I'm still young at heart and still have much to offer. I want to get back in the game and manage. Why? Because I love everything about the game. Baseball gave me my identity. Without baseball I'm a normal guy to an extent. I have a wonderful wife and a great family. I'm also learning how to be a good grandfather. But I also need a purpose outside of my family.

My significance comes when I can serve others, like helping young players to understand, respect, and appreciate the essence of baseball. My goal is to see today's players enjoy the game and have the same passion and love for baseball as I do. I just want to give back to this game I have loved and played my whole life. You see, no matter how hard you try, you just can't take away "the Kid" in me.

It breaks my heart that I'm out of baseball right now. I'm not doing what I truly believe I'm best suited for. I know the clock is ticking and my time for being considered for a job as a major league manager may be running out. I believe I have a lot to offer, and I want to give back to the game that treated me so well.

10

The Managers I Have Known

IN MY MAJOR LEAGUE PLAYING CAREER, I PLAYED FOR 11 different managers, and I learned something from each of them, knowingly and unknowingly, which I was able to apply when I started managing in the minors. In some cases, what I learned was something I wanted to avoid.

We're all the product of our experiences. It's human nature to borrow, even unwittingly, from the people to whom we are exposed: parents, teachers, clergy, employers, friends, siblings. As a manager, I even borrowed from teammates, opponents, and my own experiences as a player. I just hope I had the good sense to take the good things and filter out the not-so-good.

In some cases, what I learned was something I wanted to avoid.

Of all my managers, the one who had the greatest impact on me was Karl Kuehl, even though he managed only the first 128 games for the Expos in 1976. He had been my manager in my first two seasons in the minor leagues. I was 18 years old at the time, very impressionable, and eager to learn a new position, and Karl was more helpful to me than I could ever have imagined. His sincerity and devotion was second to none.

Karl would take me out to the field early in the day and throw tennis balls at me, trying to get me to turn the proper way at bat. As for my catching, early in my career I had a tendency to drop a lot of pitches and Karl said, "I'm going to start fining you. You need to start concentrating a little more."

Karl managed me in class AA and AAA, and in the Instructional League. He was a guy who really cared. I owe him so much that I can never repay. He's one of my closest friends to this day.

My first major league manager was Gene Mauch, who had been with the Expos for six years when I arrived to stay in 1975. Gene was renowned in baseball as a strategist. He was the "boy genius" with the Phillies in the sixties until he blew a six-and-a-half-game lead with 12 games to play in 1964. Later, he became a respected elder statesman with the Twins and Angels. Mauch managed in the major leagues for 26 seasons. When he retired, he was fourth all-time in games managed and eighth in wins. But he also was fourth all-time in games lost.

Gene's offensive philosophy was to get the first batter on base, bunt him over, play for one run, and hope your pitchers will get you through. I used some of Mauch's philosophy when I managed, but not always. Gene was a by-the-book guy and I don't believe in always going by the book. Sometimes you have to go with your hunches and manage by the seat of your pants.

Kuehl replaced Mauch in 1976 and didn't make it through the year. When he was fired, Charlie Fox took over, and the first thing he said to me was, "You'll never play the outfield again as long as I'm a part of this organization." Charlie was true to his word and I appreciated that. He managed the team for only 34 games, but he stayed on as general manager.

Dick Williams took over as Expos manager in 1977. He came in with a reputation for success. He had won a pennant with the Red Sox and three straight division titles, and two pennants and two World Series with Oakland, so he was going to get the respect and attention of his players.

Williams was one of those guys who didn't always go by the book. He often went from his gut. Under Williams, the Expos started getting better. He incorporated more speed and put on more hit-and-run plays. I loved the way Dick managed and I learned a lot of strategy from him.

Williams was upset when he didn't get a contract extension after finishing second in 1979 and 1980. He went public with his complaints against the Expos' front office and was fired with 27 games remaining in the second half of the strike-shortened 1981 season. Jim Fanning replaced Williams, finished up the '81 season, and came back to manage all of the 1982 season. Fanning wasn't your ideal manager. A nice guy, a great guy, and a good baseball man, but not what I would call a big-league manager. He was better suited for the front office—player personnel and development—not managing.

In 1983, the Expos brought in Bill Virdon, who had managed the Pirates for two years, the Yankees for two years, and the Astros for eight. Virdon was a physical fitness bug. He was in his fifties, but he had the body of a 30-year-old. He put us through running drills in spring training that made us feel like we were in Marine boot camp.

> *It didn't matter if you were a superstar or a rookie. He just wanted you to play hard.*

From Virdon, I learned about handling players. Bill was a disciplinarian who treated every player the same. It didn't matter if you were a superstar or a rookie. He just wanted you to play hard.

As a player, I prided myself on hustling at all times. But in one game I hit a ball to shallow center field that I thought was going to be caught, and I kind of lollygagged around first. I was between first and second when the ball fell in, and I had to scramble to get back to first.

Virdon confronted me. "You should have been on second base," he said.

The next day, he benched me. I had to apologize to him before he would play me again. I did, and after one day on the bench, Virdon put me back in the lineup.

The incident taught me a valuable lesson. I was swinging the bat well at the time, but in Virdon's eyes, that didn't give me a free pass. He did what he felt he had to do. Bill insisted on discipline and that earned him respect. He was a no-nonsense guy and it didn't matter who you were, he would not tolerate lack of hustle. That's something I took from him when I became a manager.

In 1985, I went to the New York Mets and the manager there was Davey Johnson, who wasn't much of a strategist or a disciplinarian as much as he was a monitor of the players. He had a way of getting the most out of his players. He was a players' manager. He'd put up a lineup and let you go out and play. He also was one of the first managers to implement the use of computers. Davey was a computer expert.

When I got to New York, I was in my thirties and I had played in more than 140 games a year in seven of the previous eight seasons, and Davey was the first manager to protect me by having me sit out day games after night games. After New York, I went to San Francisco and played for Roger Craig, who was a fun guy to be around. Roger was on top of everything. He was the first manager I played for who took over from his pitchers and catchers in controlling the running game by calling the signs himself from the dugout.

Playing for the Giants was a new experience for me, the first time I was in a platoon role. Roger made sure I always knew a few days ahead of time when I would be playing and when I would be sitting, which is very important when you're not a full-time player.

When I left the Giants, I signed with the Dodgers and played for Tommy Lasorda. That was an experience.

Tommy is a great ambassador for baseball…and for the Dodgers. Tommy may have had his favorites, especially those players who came up through the Dodgers' farm system. All those players who bled Dodger Blue became family to Lasorda.

I was frustrated because I didn't get a chance to play as much as Lasorda led me to believe I would. I was the backup to Mike Scioscia, who was one of Tommy's boys, a Dodger Blue guy, and Lasorda seemed to bend over backwards for Mike at my expense. Mind you, at the time Scioscia was making five times more money than I was and that might have had something to do with Tommy's decision.

In Lasorda's defense, when I played for him, he was going through a difficult time. His son had passed away that year and he was dealing with some heavy emotional stuff that devastated him. Also, he had a lucrative deal with the diet drink Slim Fast. According to government regulations, if you endorse a product you have to undergo periodic checks to prove you use that product. Tommy loves to eat, but if he wasn't losing weight he could lose his lucrative contract with Slim Fast. In order for Tommy to keep his weight down, Bill Buhler, the Dodgers' trainer, would take him to a pool and put a harness on him and have him swim laps.

Tommy would leave the pool and come into the clubhouse and he'd be famished. After a game, there would be the usual spread of food for the players. There were always celebrities, Tommy's friends, hanging around the clubhouse before and after games, so Tommy had the spread of food in his office, which made me a little uncomfortable.

One night a player made himself a sandwich. The player put his sandwich down and turned around for a second and when the player turned back, there was Tommy taking a big bite out of the sandwich.

I can't say playing for Lasorda was always a pleasant experience, but Tommy did call me and give me the opportunity to fulfill a dream by playing for the team I rooted for as a kid growing up in Southern California. For that, I will be forever grateful to Lasorda, who wanted me when no other manager or team was interested in my services. It was in Dodger Blue that I got the 2,000[th] hit of my career off Tom Glavine and scored my 1,000[th] run.

In my final season in Montreal, Tom Runnells was the manager, but for only 37 games. Then Felipe Alou came along, and I really liked playing for him. His strategy was a lot like Gene Mauch's. He put on the hit-and-run every now and then, he used the bunt, and he was excellent with the pitching staff. Felipe was always aware of what was happening on the field. It amazed me how he could be talking to a coach on the bench and giving a sign to the third-base coach at the same time.

> *I can't say playing for Lasorda was always a pleasant experience, but Tommy did…give me the opportunity to fulfill a dream by playing for the team I rooted for as a kid…*

When I became a manager, I had all this experience with all these managers with different personalities and different philosophies from which to draw. It was up to me to pick and choose what I learned from each of them and formulate my own style. I took a little bit of Gene Mauch, a little bit of Bill Virdon, a lot of Karl Kuehl, and I took some of the fun of Roger Craig, a little bit of Davey Johnson, and finished with a little bit of Felipe Alou.

With all that and my own playing experience from 18 years as a catcher, I thought I could manage a major league team. I still do. But I keep running into roadblocks. People find reasons not to give me my shot. When I talked to general managers who had a managing vacancy, they'd tell me I had to get managing experience. But the Mets hired Willie Randolph and he didn't have managing experience. The Marlins hired Joe Girardi and he didn't have managing experience.

Then I heard that the reason I wasn't getting a chance was that Hall of Famers don't make good managers. They're too demanding. Things came so easy for them as players that they have a hard time accepting the failures of players.

Well, look at how many Hall of Famers got their shot as managers: Yogi Berra, Mickey Cochrane, Eddie Collins, Gabby Hartnett, Walter Johnson, Frank Robinson, Ted Williams, Bob Lemon, Christy Mathewson. True, they weren't all good managers, but some of them were successful.

A lot of guys are hired as managers simply because they managed before. No matter that they were unsuccessful, they had managing experience. There's an old boys' network in baseball. Once you get in the club, you have a chance to be recycled and get another job. Art Howe was fired by the Mets, and then the Texas Rangers hired Ron Washington, who was a coach for Howe in Oakland. The first thing Washington did was hire Howe to be his bench coach.

I figured I had to somehow get myself inducted into that old boys' network. All right, if I need managing experience, I thought, I'll remove that barrier by going to the minor leagues to manage, which I did. Maybe I could move up to Triple A, the next stop before the major leagues. Maybe I'd land a job as a major league coach. But even after my efforts, still nothing.

I'm not giving up. I know I can do it. I've thought a lot about managing in the major leagues, and I know what I'll do if I ever get the chance.

When it comes to managing a major league team, dealing with the media is the number-one priority, depending on what city you're in. Obviously, New York is the media capital of the world, so there I believe it's important to be available for a lot of things the club needs you to do, such as representing the team at various functions and promoting the team.

Where strategy is concerned, managing in the majors is no different from managing in the minors. That's the easy part. The game doesn't change. The game will run itself. It's hitting, throwing, running, pitching, catching. I know strategy like the back of my hand. I know when to put on bunt plays, when to hit and run, when a player needs a rest, how to motivate a player to get him going.

> *That's the easy part. The game doesn't change.*

You're managing a team, but you're also managing individual personalities. A manager has to know each player, what motivates him, what makes him tick. There's a way to handle each player and to inspire him. With some guys you can get in their face and tell them they're not doing something right. Others you have to treat with kid gloves. It's a matter of how you handle each individual and how to get the most out of him. I

It's a matter of how you handle each individual and how to get the most out of him.

believe the best way to do that is to show how much you care about the players, how much you believe in them.

Players will test a manager occasionally, but I believe they're like your children in many ways: they'll try to get away with things, but down deep, they really crave discipline and direction.

On the field, pitching is most important. It needs to be monitored and understood. A manager has to rely heavily on his pitching coach; it has to be a hands-on situation between manager and pitching coach. When to get a pitcher up in the bullpen. Who's available for that day's game and who isn't. How to tell when a pitcher is out of gas and needs to be replaced. A manager has to earn the trust of his pitchers. If pitchers don't trust the manager, they will lose respect for him.

A manager has to protect his players. He has to fight for his players. When I managed, I was the first one out there if one of my players got into an argument with an umpire. I saved ejections and fines for many of my players. If players know the manager is going to fight for them, the manager earns their respect. They know the manager has their back.

Bobby Cox is great at that. That's why he has broken the all-time record for getting thrown out of games. If one of his players gets into an argument with an umpire, Bobby is right out there to voice his opinion and protect his player. Players respect that.

On the other hand, Cox doesn't let his players get away with anything. I saw it when I was broadcasting. One day the Braves were in town, and Chipper Jones came out for batting practice wearing something different from what every other player was wearing. Cox sent him back into the clubhouse to change. It didn't matter to Bobby that Chipper was the Braves' biggest star.

Andruw Jones used to wear his hat backward. Cox changed that.

For years, Ken Griffey Jr. wore his hat backwards and got away with it. I would never allow that. I don't care who you are, you have to respect the game.

> *A manager has to protect his players. He has to fight for his players.*

A manager can usually tell if a player is giving 100 percent. If not, what you need to do is nip that in the bud without showing up that player. If I needed to yell at somebody, I would do it behind closed doors. I wouldn't do it in front of the team. However, if I had to address the whole team, I might pick out certain individuals to show that I wasn't playing favorites. A manager who showed that to the whole team, no matter who they were, proved that he cared. What I tried to emphasize was that I could criticize them, yell at them, but then I also showed them how much I cared about them.

Joe Torre is a stoic individual, but he has a lot of respect. He has good people around him for coaches, so he can kind of sit back and let his coaches take care of things for him. If you hear him in interviews, he's outstanding. You see it in how he interacts with superstars like Alex Rodriguez and Derek Jeter, who likes to kid with Joe by calling him "Mr. Torre."

When I played for Davey Johnson, there were certain individuals he didn't have to get on because he knew they were going to play hard for him. But certain other guys Davey came down on because he had to prove to everybody else that he wasn't going to allow them to get away with anything.

If a guy plays hard for you every day, you might show him some leniency. But that would be nothing more than, on a hot day in spring training, telling a player, "Hey, why don't you take it on in for the rest of the day? You've earned it." That's not giving in totally.

Time is the big issue. If you designate a time for players to be there and someone shows up late, that's showing lack of respect. If a player is there on time and looks like he's dragging, but he's a guy who plays hard, you might give him some time off. That's the privilege. It's relatively minor, but if the guy hasn't given you any problems, you might say, "Hey, do you want to take batting practice today?"

As a hypothetical, if I were a manager, how would I deal with a player like Barry Bonds, a guy who marches to his own beat? A lot of people dislike him. He's very arrogant. He's his own guy, and he has created his own domain in the clubhouse, where he has his own lounge chair in his private little corner. He tends to alienate his teammates by distancing himself from everybody else. It's like he thinks he's bigger than the game.

When he was going after the home-run record, he obviously had to play, but good communication was necessary because he was having shin splints for a while.

As his manager, you had to ask, "Barry, how do you feel? Do you feel like playing today?"

No question, he's one guy you have to treat differently. After all, he is in his forties. You handle him the best way you can, but you also know he's going to get away with more than anybody because of his age and what he has accomplished.

You can't bench him for lack of hustle. Because of the shift against him, he'll hit a bullet to somebody and just coast down to first base. In the outfield, for all the Gold Gloves he has won, he doesn't move around like he used to. Again, that's because of his age. He's one guy you'd have to treat with kid gloves.

If he showed up late, I would have a problem with that. But I think he would know better. If you have to make a point, then you have to make a point in order to gain the respect of all. If you let one guy go, regardless of his status, it creates friction among the entire team.

So there you have my ideas, my philosophies of managing. I'm just waiting for a chance to implement those philosophies. I don't understand a system that doesn't want someone who has been successful in a game, is a Hall of Famer, can represent a ballclub, can handle the press—all the criteria that everyone agrees are necessary for a big-league manager to be successful.

And yet I'm realistic enough to know that the chance may never come.

I believe God has a plan for me. Each of us is put on this earth for a reason. I think there's a calling in all of us. People tell me I have so much to offer in the game as a manager. They say that's where I need to be.

Each of us is put on this earth for a reason. I think there's a calling in all of us.

What if there are no offers to manage a major league team? Then what do I do? I've thought about coaching in a major college program. I would be receptive to that. I think that would be outstanding. I would find that very rewarding, and it also would get my competitive juices flowing, which I crave and which I miss. If that doesn't happen, then I'll get more involved in the community, play in some golf tournaments, and continue my work with my foundation.

For now, I'm just going to be in a waiting mode and accept that I am wherever God needs me to be. But I still feel where I need to be is managing a big-league team because when I put that uniform back on and started managing, the kid in me really came out.

11

Making It into the Hall

IN 1998, FIVE FULL YEARS AFTER I RETIRED AS A PLAYER, my name appeared on the Hall of Fame ballot for the first time. I was encouraged when 200 voting members of the Baseball Writers Association of America included me on their ballots, the fifth highest vote total that year behind Don Sutton, who was elected, and Tony Perez, who just missed, Ron Santo, and Jim Rice.

While I had high hopes that I would someday be voted into the Hall of Fame, I really didn't expect it to happen the first year I was eligible. Yogi Berra, Roy Campanella, Mickey Cochrane, and Gabby Hartnett weren't elected in their first years.

For a player to be elected, he must receive 75 percent of the votes cast. My percentage that year was 42.3, which left me 155 votes short of election. Some longtime voters told me my showing the first time out was a good indication I would eventually make it. They said it was customary for a player's vote total to increase after his first year on the ballot.

My hopes were dashed the following year when my vote total decreased and I lost 32 votes. Why was I going backward? Gee, I must have had a bad year in 1999. What made my showing even more inexplicable was that Carlton Fisk was on the ballot for the first time, and he polled 330 votes, and deservedly so. He missed election by only 44 votes, which meant he probably was going to make it in the near future. I respected Pudge a great deal, but at the same time I was perplexed over my decline. Fisk and I were contemporaries. Our careers paralleled one another. Our numbers were very similar. Judge for yourself:

	GAMES	HITS	HOME RUNS	RBI	AVERAGE
Fisk	2,499	2,356	376	1,330	.269
Carter	2,296	2,092	324	1,225	.262

Almost identical, as you can see. Pudge and I also are two of only four catchers in baseball history—the others are Yogi Berra and Johnny Bench—with 2,000 hits, 1,000 runs scored, 300 home runs, and 1,200 RBIs. With all that, it was difficult for me to understand why my vote total was decreasing.

For years, the question was who is better, Fisk or Carter? The debate usually got resolved diplomatically with the answer: Fisk in the American League, Carter in the National League.

When neither of us was elected in 1999, I thought it would be appropriate for the two of us to get in in the same year. But in the 2000 election, Fisk got 397 votes and was elected, and, although my vote total jumped from 168 to 248, I still was only at 49.7 percent and short of election by 137 votes.

I was happy for Fisk, who is very deserving of being in the Hall of Fame, but I began to wonder what was going on in my case. What did I do—or what didn't I do—that my vote total was still below 50 percent? As it turned out, Pudge's election actually helped me because it called attention to the simi-

What did I do—or what didn't I do—that my vote total was still below 50 percent?

larity of our careers. Baseball writers around the country started writing, "Hey, what about Gary Carter? He was recognized as the best of his era, but here's Fisk getting in the Hall of Fame. Doesn't Carter deserve to be in?"

I missed out again in 2001, but at least my vote total was moving up. Dave Winfield and Kirby Puckett were elected that year, and I was third with 334 votes, 64.9 percent. People kept telling me it was only a matter of time.

In December 2001, after the Hall of Fame ballots had been sent out, Dale Petroskey, the president of the Hall of Fame, flew down to Florida on the private plane of Hall of Fame Chairman of the Board Jane Forbes Clark and visited me at the office of the Gary Carter Foundation. He said he had good vibes that I would be elected that year, my fifth year on the ballot. Mind you, Petroskey had no inside information. The Baseball Writers count the ballots with the aid of an independent auditor and not even executives of the Hall of Fame get any advance notice about the election. But Dale has been involved with the process for some years, and I figured he had pretty good insight into the thinking of the voters.

After listening to Dale, Sandy and I got our hopes up very high. If the president of the Hall of Fame thought my chances were good, that buoyed our spirits. Ozzie Smith was on the ballot for the first time in 2002 and I began to think of how cool it would be for me to go in with "the Wizard," a guy who stole so many base hits from me. I celebrated in advance by buying new cars for Sandy and me.

A month after Petroskey's visit, the vote came out. In anticipation of my election, my house was overrun with local press, local TV, all waiting for the phone call. But the call never came. Ozzie made it easily, but my vote total was 343, 72.7 percent, 11 votes short of election. I started thinking, "Maybe it's not meant to be."

Although I was getting closer, and I knew I still had 10 years of eligibility remaining, I was becoming anxious because my dad's health was failing and I wanted so much for him to be around if and when I was elected.

On the other hand, as disappointing as it was that I fell 11 votes short, it probably was a blessing in disguise that I wasn't elected that year because our daughter Christy had set the date for her wedding, and it was July 13, 2002. The Hall of Fame induction that year was two weeks later, so it would have been chaos making arrangements for all the people I wanted to be in Cooperstown and for the wedding.

We had family from Washington, Oregon, and California all coming to the Hall of Fame induction and the wedding.

Obviously, we would have worked it out if we had to, but it would have been hectic.

When the 2003 vote came along, my sixth year of eligibility, I made a decision. I was not going to get my hopes up. I was not going to make any preparations. I wasn't even going to make myself available for interviews. All I did was comply with Jack O'Connell, the

When the 2003 vote came along, my sixth year of eligibility, I made a decision. I was not going to get my hopes up.

secretary-treasurer of the Baseball Writers Association of America, by giving him my cell phone number as he requested of all the leading candidates.

On the day of the 2003 announcement, I went to play golf accompanied by my wife, Sandy, and my close friends Tommy Hutton, Ray Strickland, Phil Mendence, and Mead Chasky.

We had just finished the 18th hole when I got the call from O'Connell, who said, "Kid, you're in."

I shouted, "*Yeah!*"

Believe it or not, O'Connell's call came in at 12:08 PM. I know that because as soon as he heard me shout, Phil Mendence looked at his watch. I had my first birdie of the day on the 8th hole and I shot an 80 and I received 78 percent of the vote. All those eights on this special day. The date was January 7, but it must have been January 8 somewhere in the world.

Eddie Murray, in his first year of eligibility, also was elected. I received 387 votes. I made it just barely, by 15 votes. That doesn't matter. It was enough to get me in, one

All those eights on this special day. The date was January 7, but it must have been January 8 somewhere in the world.

of only 13 catchers (plus three from the Negro Leagues) to be elected to the Hall of Fame. Once you're elected, nobody asks you how close the vote was. You're in or you're not.

When I was elected, the people of the Hall of Fame told me that I would be going in as a Montreal Expo. I had no choice. I don't know for certain how I would have chosen if I did have a choice. I won a World Series with the Mets and probably got more national recognition playing in New York, the media capital of the world, than I did in Montreal. But I played longer with the Expos, who retired my No. 8.

I asked Dale Petroskey if they could split the hat and have the Expos on one side and the Mets on the other, but he turned down that idea. There are only two players in the Hall of Fame who do not have a team logo on their plaque. Yogi Berra's cap is turned backward and Catfish Hunter has a generic hat because he couldn't decide between the Oakland Athletics and the New York Yankees. But that was before the Hall of Fame stepped in and took the decision away from the players.

At one time the Hall of Fame inductee chose which team he wanted to represent. Eventually, that caused players to put it up to the highest bidder. There are examples of inductees choosing the team they represent in the Hall of Fame in exchange for jobs. The Hall's people loathed the practice and decreed that they would avoid it becoming a monetary issue by deciding unilaterally, based on length of service, which team's hat would be depicted on a player's plaque.

At first I questioned the Hall of Fame's putting me in as an Expo. My argument was that if the Expos were contracted, or if they moved, who was going to remember the Montreal Expos 25 years up the road?

They came back by saying they wanted the Expos' place in history to be acknowledged, and, unless Andre Dawson eventually gets elected, I'll be the only one in the Hall of Fame with an Expos cap on his plaque.

Because of that, I said part of my induction speech in French and acknowledged the fans in Montreal. I later found out that they stopped the game briefly in Olympic Stadium and showed the induction ceremonies on the big screen, which was kind of neat. The Expos are due their place in baseball history, but for my sake, I have an association in the Hall of Fame with a team that's no longer in existence. I guess I may end up being the only Expo in the team's 36-year history that will be remembered in Cooperstown. What is a shame is that Montreal was a great city.

> *The Expos are due their place in baseball history, but for my sake, I have an association in the Hall of Fame with a team that's no longer in existence.*

In the long run, however, I'm glad the decision was taken out of my hands because if I had to make a choice between the Mets and the Expos, I was certain to alienate the fans of the team I didn't choose.

• • •

The afternoon of my election, we celebrated with a few friends at a local restaurant. When we got home, all of a sudden, friends, family, and neighbors began showing up to offer their congratulations. There must have been more than 35 people there, and we hadn't invited one of them. People just started showing up once the word got out. Local television reporters and camera crews showed up and I did several interviews. The telephone never stopped ringing the whole night.

Once I was voted in, I started on a whirlwind tour that lasted the better part of a year and, to some degree, is still going on to this day.

I have heard many people, in and out of the Hall of Fame, say that once you're elected, your life changes dramatically. I can attest to that. Once I was voted in, I started on a whirlwind tour that lasted the better part of a year and, to some degree, is still going on to this day. In some ways, it might have been a blessing that I didn't get that job managing the Yankees' Columbus farm team.

The first order of business was for Sandy and me to fly to New York for the press conference announcing my election. Jeff Wilpon was at the press conference representing the Mets, and I told him I had no choice in which cap was going to appear on my plaque. Jeff said, "Don't worry about it. You'll always be a Met."

The day after the announcement, Sandy and I flew back home, and then a couple of days later, we returned to New York for the whirlwind tour, a couple of autograph signings, appearances on *Good Morning America* and the *Late Show with David Letterman*—all of it arranged by

Mead Chasky, who orchestrated everything. I owe him such a debt of gratitude. He was a tower of strength and a lifesaver. He took over the job of organizing and making arrangements and accommodations in Cooperstown for my many friends and family members.

We sent out invitations to everybody. Mead had a list of names, addresses, and telephone numbers of those we invited to the induction. He also organized a party a couple of nights before the induction in a private room at the Pines Restaurant in Cooperstown. More than 100 people were at the party, including friends, former teammates, and family members from all over the country, even cousins I hadn't seen in years. People were coming out of the woodwork. I owe a lot to George Wafer who was instrumental in making the party a success, and to Mead. I don't know how I would have managed without them.

Later that summer, the Mets honored me at Shea Stadium and gave me a Harley-Davidson motorcycle, something I always wanted. I have to say the Mets have been very good to me. In 2000, they asked me to throw out the first pitch in a World Series game against the Yankees. I brought my son, D.J., with me and he had a great time. He got to meet actors Jack Nicholson and Tim Robbins, who were there that day, and he had his picture taken with Marc Anthony, who sang the national anthem, and with two Yankees D.J.s, Derek Jeter and David Justice.

In 2001, the Mets inducted me into their Hall of Fame, a great honor, and in 2006, they flew my whole family and Jesse Orosco's family to New York for Opening Day. Before the game, Jesse and I reenacted the final pitch from the 1986 World Series as part of a 20th anniversary celebration of the Mets' last World Series championship.

After the Hall of Fame induction, the Expos invited us to Montreal and honored me before a game at Olympic Stadium, which turned out to be a special day. They presented me with a cruise for two, a painting of Montreal by a great artist, and an artist's rendering of a catcher's mask with my likeness on it. Every fan attending the game received an 8" x 10" picture of me and a commemorative coin with my picture engraved on it. Between innings, they showed filmed highlights of my career with the Expos. It was a very classy event.

The Expos' general manager at the time happened to be Omar Minaya, who sent me a beautiful letter thanking me for being part of the ceremony.

• • •

The first call I made after I got the news that I had been elected to the Hall of Fame was to my dad, who was 84 years old and in poor health. He had been so instrumental in my baseball career. He was my coach in Little League, Pony League, and American Legion. He patted me on the back when I was a boy, and he lived through my career as a professional.

He patted me on the back when I was a boy and he lived through my career as a professional.

Sandy had a huge surprise party planned for me on the night of Saturday, January 25, but on Wednesday, January 22, the day before we were scheduled to leave New York and return to Florida, I got a call from my brother, who told me, "Dad's not doing too well. They took him to the hospital, but I think he's going to be okay."

We left New York on Thursday morning, January 23, and by the time the plane landed in Florida, my brother had left another message asking me to call him. He said, "Dad has taken a turn for the worse."

The doctors realized his heart was failing, and they were prepping him for a pacemaker. While they were prepping him for the operating room, his blood pressure dropped drastically. I asked my brother, "Gordy, is he going to be okay?"

"He's stable, and he's coherent," my brother said. "He's doing okay right now."

After I talked to my brother, Sandy came into my den and she was crying.

"Honey," I said. "What's wrong?"

She said, "I didn't want to tell you, but I've got to tell you. I have this big party planned for you, but I think you need to go see your father."

Sandy said, 'I have such a feeling. I know you need to go. I have a premonition.'

I said, "No, no, Gordy said he's all right."

Sandy said, "I have such a feeling. I know you need to go. I have a premonition."

That's when Sandy told me that people were coming from all over the country for the surprise party. Karl Kuehl was coming from Arizona; my brother and his wife were coming from California; Andre Dawson, Jerry Royster, Tommy Hutton, and Mike Schmidt were coming. The

Mets had graciously sent her a tape of highlights of my career that she planned to show at the party.

This was Thursday night. We went to bed with the party still on. At 6:00 the next morning, the phone rang and it was my dad's nurse. She said, "You need to come now."

I had nothing packed, no airline ticket, nothing. What do I do? There was a flight leaving at 7:00 AM and Sandy said, "You're never going to make it."

I said, "I'll make it."

I threw some things in an overnight bag and jumped in the car, and Sandy drove me to the airport. It was about 6:35 when she dropped me off, and I was still without a ticket. The people at Delta knew me because I had been flying so often. They got me through security—and this was only a year and a half after 9/11—and I made the flight. I was the last one on the plane.

Sandy went back home and called all the people who were coming to the party to tell them I had to fly to California because my father had taken a turn for the worse and the party was canceled. Then she took a noon flight and joined me in California.

I got to the hospital, and my dad was on life support. He had been considered a "code blue" three times that day. He couldn't communicate, but I held his hand and said, "Dad, if you can hear me, squeeze my hand." He was able to do that, so he knew I was there.

After a while, the priest said, "You can't do anything more for him." We left the hospital a little after 9:00 PM on Friday, January 24. We got a call at 12:20 Saturday morning and were told to hurry to the hospital. We arrived at 12:40 AM and received the message that my dad had just passed. His funeral was held in the same funeral home that took care of my mother when she died 37 years before.

I'm sad that Dad didn't live long enough to make it to Cooperstown for the induction ceremonies, but I take comfort in the fact that at least he lived long enough to know I had been elected to the Hall of Fame.

12

The Baseball Tradition

I'M A BASEBALL FAN, ALWAYS HAVE BEEN AND ALWAYS WILL be. I still follow the game closely, on and off the field. I'm aware of baseball's history and tradition, of the players who came decades before me and of those playing today.

Baseball is the greatest game ever created. It has stood the test of time. While other sports have undergone many rule changes, baseball has remained basically the same game on the field for more than 100 years: nine innings, three outs per side, four balls, three strikes.

Baseball is the greatest game ever created. It has stood the test of time.

In football, for example, they moved the goal posts from the front of the end zone to 10 yards deep in the end zone, and they moved the kickoff from the 40-yard line to the 35-yard line, and now the 30-yard line. In basketball, they introduced the shot clock and the three-point line and widened the three-second lane. All of these rule changes were a concession to the fact that the playing area had shrunk because people are bigger, stronger, and faster now than they were 50 years ago.

Baseball players also are bigger, stronger, and faster today than they were 50 years ago, but the distance from the pitcher to the batter remains at 60 feet, six inches, and the distance between the bases remains at 90 feet. And it still works. The shortstop still has time to throw a batter out on a ground ball in the hole.

Baseball is the only sport played without a clock. In football, for example, if a team is leading by five touchdowns with two or three minutes to play, the team behind has no chance. In basketball, if a team is up by 30 or 40 points with a few minutes remaining, it's impossible for the trailing team to catch up. In baseball, theoretically, no lead is insurmountable. Baseball is the only game in which there are no turnovers that allow the defense to score. In baseball, each team is allotted 27 outs and, therefore, each has an equal opportunity to score. In football, one team may run off 50 or 60 plays while its opponent runs off 20 or 30 plays. In basketball, one team may take 70 or 80 shots while its opponent is held to 30 or 40 shots.

Baseball is also the only sport that does not permit unlimited substitution. Unlike football, basketball, and hockey, once a baseball player is removed from a game, he's gone for good.

Baseball's critics say the game is too slow, and it's dull. To that I say baseball is meant to be slow. It was designed to be played on warm, summer days. A day on the beach is slow. A picnic is slow. Both are enjoyable. Chess is slow. Is it dull? Not to Bobby Fischer it isn't.

In answer to those who say baseball is dull, this is what the great sportswriter Red Smith once said: "Baseball is dull only to people with dull minds."

I like football, basketball, hockey, and golf, too. I admire the strength and skill of professional football players, the athleticism of professional basketball players, the precision of hockey players, the endless amount of time golfers spend practicing. But I prefer baseball because it's a game where a guy like Freddie Patek, who stood 5'5" and weighed about 145 pounds, can have a successful 14-year major league career, and a pitcher like Ron Guidry, who weighed 160 pounds, can throw the ball in the mid-nineties, strike out 18 batters in a game (the California Angels), and have a 25–3 record for the Yankees in 1978.

I also prefer baseball because it's a more cerebral game than football and basketball. Baseball makes you think. I love watching the moves and countermoves of opposing managers and the thought process of the pitcher and catcher trying to outguess a hitter and, conversely, a hitter trying to outguess the pitcher and catcher. As a former catcher, that is the part of the game I miss most.

I also prefer baseball because it's a more cerebral game than football and basketball. Baseball makes you think.

As much as I love baseball, I admit the game is not without its faults and its problems. Some of what I see today I like. Some of it disturbs my sensibilities and my sense of order. The fact is I am a traditionalist when it comes to baseball and that tradition is being tampered with.

I began to see sweeping changes in the game off the field in the early 1990s. It actually started in 1989, when first Kirby Puckett and then Orel Hershiser became baseball's first $3 million players. It was just about that time that the game became more of a business than it ever was. New ballparks were being built mainly to accommodate corporations with plush luxury boxes that would bring increased revenue.

Since 1990, 20 new major league ballparks have been built with four more on the planning board. When those four are completed and opened, 24 of the 30 major league teams will be playing in ballparks that opened since 1990, all of them state of the art, all of them catering to the creature comfort of fans, and all of them with opulent, exclusive, revenue-producing luxury boxes.

Baseball faced a serious crisis in 1994 with a labor dispute that forced cancellation of half the season and all of the postseason. The strike threw the game into turmoil and prompted baseball's leaders to try to figure out how the all-American game—baseball, apple pie, Chevrolet— was going to recapture the interest of the fan.

Baseball found the answer to the problem perhaps inadvertently. Fast-forward to 1998, when the game enjoyed a resurgence, the impetus for which was the challenge to Roger Maris's single-season home-run record of 61 set in 1961, by Mark McGwire, who blasted 70 homers, and Sammy Sosa, who belted 66.

Suddenly, fans turned out in droves, and since that season, baseball has enjoyed its greatest growth in attendance. Fans like home runs. They like offense. They like a lot of scoring. Fans want to see the high-scoring game. They don't want to see pitching duels with scores of 1–0 and 2–1. They'd rather see home runs and the great home-run hitters. As proof of the appeal the home run has

Fans like home runs. They like offense. They like a lot of scoring.

for fans, the ball McGwire hit for his 70th home run was sold to a collector for $3.5 million.

Baseball's leaders got the message the fans were sending them. What followed were changes in the game designed to benefit the hitter, encourage home runs, and penalize the pitcher. Baseballs were wound tighter, the strike zone shrunk, expansion diluted the talent of pitching, and the 11 new ballparks that opened since 1998 had shorter, more reachable fences. (Another factor was the steroid issue, which I will get into later in the book.)

Look at how the All-Star Game has become such a spectacular event in the past few years with the home-run-hitting contest, the Legends Game, and the Futures Game. My last All-Star Game was in 1988. Back then we went to the city where the game was being played, a luncheon was held for the All-Stars the day before the game, then we played the game and left immediately after. That's it.

Today, it's a three-day affair with all kinds of events going on. The home-run-hitting contest has become as big as the game itself. In the 2007 All-Star Game in San Francisco, they charged $200 per ticket for the home-run-hitting contest, and it was sold out.

After they played a tie in the 2002 All-Star Game, baseball decided that it had to put more juice into the game and make it more meaningful for players and fans. Thereafter, at stake in the All-Star Game would be the extra home-field advantage in the World Series. It would go to the competing team representing the league that won the All-Star Game. Commissioner Bud Selig made a big deal out of it, and MLB adopted the slogan, "This time it counts."

There was a pride factor where the National League tried to prevail over the American League, and vice versa. I was always told how important it was and what it meant to represent your league.

Well, when I played, the All-Star Game always counted. It meant something to the players. There was a pride factor, where the National League tried to prevail over the American League, and vice versa. I was always told how important it was and what it meant to represent your league. When I was a young player and played in my first All-Star Game, you heard it in the clubhouse from older players like Pete Rose and Johnny Bench and Mike Schmidt. To them it wasn't an exhibition or a three-day party, which it was to many players. They wanted to win, and they played the game to win for the pride and honor of the National League.

I was elected to 11 All-Star teams. I played in 10 All-Star Games for the National League, and we won eight of them, including a streak of five straight. It was a matter of pride.

I always felt that way about All-Star Games. I'm proud to say I have a collection of Most Valuable Player awards from those games. In 1973, I hit two home runs, went

4-for-4, and was voted MVP in the Eastern League All-Star Game. I was also MVP in the 1981 and 1984 major league All-Star Games. In 2006, I was MVP of the Legends Game and the winning manager in the Futures Game, which puts on display the best players in the minor leagues. It's sort of an audition to familiarize fans with the game's stars of the future.

Two examples of how the hitter is being pampered at the expense of the pitcher are that pitchers are dissuaded from pitching inside and hitters go to bat wearing so much armor they look like the cast of a movie about the knights of King Arthur's day.

If a pitcher tries to pitch inside, he faces the risk of being ejected or fined, or both. I came up at the end of an era when there were pitchers who believed they owned the inside part of the plate. Today's hitters will hit a home run, and then they'll stand at the plate and watch the flight of the ball or style going around the bases. Pitchers like Don Drysdale, Juan Marichal, and Bob Gibson would never tolerate that sort of posing.

If you hit a home run off Bob Gibson, you had better run around those bases as fast as you could or else you better be alert the next time you came to bat because he'd knock you on your fanny. Drysdale was that way and so was Marichal.

In 1998, when McGwire hit 70 home runs and Sosa hit 66, I don't remember either of them ever being knocked down.

I never hit against Drysdale or Marichal, but I did hit against Gibson. It was Opening Day in St. Louis in

1975, Gibson's last year. He was coming off a broken leg, and he still wasn't 100 percent (he would finish with a very un-Gibson-like record of 3–10). I got two hits off him. I don't remember if they were bloops or line drives. Years later, when I ran into Gibson, I kidded him about that.

"You took me deep twice?" he said. He was mad about it. This was years after he retired, but he was angry thinking I had hit two home runs off him. That's the kind of competitor he was.

I said, "No, Gibby, I just got two singles off you."

Wearing that kind of padding removes the fear factor, allowing hitters to crowd the plate.

The padding that guys like Barry Bonds and Gary Sheffield and others wear these days is a joke. That wasn't permitted in my day. I would have gone up to bat with that stuff too if I could have. Wearing that kind of padding removes the fear factor, allowing hitters to crowd the plate.

In 1983, when I was with the Expos, I was hit on my elbow three times in a week, and I had tendinitis in my elbow so bad, I couldn't lift a carton of milk without feeling pain. All I wore on my elbow was some sort of elastic protector to try to keep it a little tighter, which was hardly any protection at all. After I got hit the third time I said, "That's it. The next guy who hits me on the elbow I'm going to go out to the mound after him."

When Rick Sutcliffe hit me on the elbow, right on the funny bone, I abandoned my plan to charge the mound because it hurt so much I couldn't even lift my arm. I just went meekly down to first base.

Pitching inside is one way pitchers are able to control the batter and maintain a fair strike zone. Without it, batters are given too much of an advantage. I'd like to see the return of the inside pitch to keep the batters honest.

13

Ch-Ch-Ch-Changes!

THE CHANGES IN BASEBALL THAT I DISCUSSED IN CHAPTER 12 have come about for one reason: money. Baseball is big business and the game is money-driven now more than ever. It is much more glamorized. It's more entertainment and showmanship today, and the tail that wags the dog is television.

You can trace this new era to Alex Rodriguez breaking the barrier by signing that record 10-year, $252 million contract with the Texas Rangers in 2001. Look at where the game has gone monetarily in the past 20 years, from Orel Hershiser and Kirby Puckett becoming the first $3 million ballplayers in 1989, to Bobby Bonilla's four-year, $28 million contract with the New York Mets in 1992, to A-Rod's average annual salary of more than $25 million.

> *Baseball is big business and the game is money-driven now more than ever.*

Teams are handing out multimillion-dollar contracts to average players these days, and the number of players making in excess of $10 million a year is staggering.

The impetus for all of these big-money contracts has been television. Teams make so much money from the FOX network's Saturday *Game of the Week* and ESPN's *Sunday Night Baseball*, along with their own regional television contracts, that they can afford to dole out these astronomical salaries. That's good for the players, and, to some degree, it has also been good for the game. But there's a down side, too.

Big-market teams like the Yankees with the YES Network and the Mets with SNY have their own television networks. The Cubs have superstation WGN, the Atlanta Braves have TBS and TNT, and the Dodgers have a rich television contract. That's why those teams are able to pay big bucks for free agents. The downside is that small-market teams like Cincinnati, Kansas City, Tampa Bay, Pittsburgh, and Minnesota, without such lucrative television contracts, can't keep up with the Joneses; they can't compete with the giants, and that creates an inequity that is regrettable.

I don't think that's good for the game. Parity is important, and if you look at the standings, there is some form of parity. Teams such as the Arizona Diamondbacks and the Florida Marlins can still win the World Series, but it's rare and difficult for those teams to sustain that success over a long period of time because they don't have the luxury of the extra money from cable television to spend on players. They have to do it with shrewd trades and superior scouting.

Players will go where the money is, and how can you blame them? How could Barry Zito turn down $126 million to leave the Oakland Athletics and sign with the San Francisco Giants?

But money doesn't guarantee a good team. Management has to make good decisions. Take Mike Hampton, for example. He signed with the Colorado Rockies for $123 million, but was traded to the Marlins and then to the Braves, then hurt his arm and had to undergo Tommy John surgery. Those big-money deals don't always pan out. But if a big-market team like the Yankees signs a Carl Pavano for $40 million and it doesn't work out, it has the resources to dump him and spend more money to sign his replacement.

> *But money doesn't guarantee a good team. Management has to make good decisions.*

Television influences the game in other ways as well. Today's players have a *SportsCenter* mentality. If a player does something spectacular, or something comical, or makes a blunder, you can turn on the television and see that play over and over. How many times does that play pop up on "Web Gems" or "That's Nasty"? Players watch those shows and that's why you see all those celebrations, the handshakes, the posing at the plate to watch the flight of a ball after it's hit, the curtain calls. Kids watch those shows, too, and they emulate the big leaguers. All that does is perpetuate the practice.

To afford the huge salaries, teams are also heavy into merchandising, such as the sale of team jerseys and caps, not only in this country but worldwide. That explains the revival of the "throwback" uniforms and why some teams wear a variety of caps and jerseys in different color combinations. The more variations of caps and jerseys they wear, the more they sell. And the more prestigious the team, the more their caps and jerseys are in demand.

How many No. 2 Yankees jerseys do you see in New York because of Derek Jeter? Or No. 5 Mets jerseys because of David Wright? Or No. 7 because of Jose Reyes? Teams are making a fortune in merchandising.

All this traces to Michael Jordan. When he left basketball to play minor league baseball, instead of wearing the familiar No. 23 that he wore with the Chicago Bulls, he wore No. 45 in baseball. Then when he returned to the Bulls, he switched from his famous No. 23 and wore No. 45 with the Bulls, so then everybody had to have a No. 45 Bulls jersey.

Another way television has influenced the game is in the glut of statistics they throw at you these days. They have statistics for everything. I started noticing that toward the end of my career, when computers first began to be used in baseball. When we had a meeting to go over the scouting report on an opposing team, they hit us with thousands of statistics. If you throw a pitch to Player A in this zone, he hits it to left field. If you throw it in that zone, he hits it to right field. They'll tell you a hitter's average against Pitcher A and his average against Pitcher B, what he bats in day games and what he bats in night games, what he bats on Monday, on Tuesday, and on Wednesday. It's ridiculous.

Scouting has become so much more sophisticated. Modern technology and video aids have taken over in major league clubhouses. A batter will make an out, and

My speech at Shea Stadium during the Mets Hall of Fame induction ceremony on August 12, 2001. Left to right are: Steve Phillips (GM), me, Gary Thorne (MC), Bob Murphy (Mets radio announcer), and Bobby Ojeda.

My son D.J. and me at Shea Stadium for the Mets '86 Reunion of the World Champions.

Me, my father, and my brother, Gordon, at my daughter Christy's rehearsal dinner in July 2002. This photo was taken six months before my father passed away.

The Little League field I played on as a kid is now named after my father.

My good friend Tommy Hutton and me celebrating just after it was announced I'd made the Hall of Fame. The day included a round of golf with Tommy, Phil Mendence, and Ray Strickland.

Ray Strickland (far left) and Phil Mendence (far right) were also with me the day my acceptance into the Hall of Fame was announced. Also pictured here are my two sons-in-law, Matt (to my right) and Kyle (to my left).

Johnny Bench and I paired together for the Hall of Fame Golf Tournament. Johnny was my role model for catching and I learned a lot about the position from watching him.

Gathered in Cooperstown, New York, for the Baseball Hall of Fame induction are (from left to right): me, Mike Schmidt, Johnny Bench, George Brett, Charley Pride, Paul Molitor, Brooks Robinson, and Harmon Killebrew.

Eddie Murray and I were inducted into the Baseball Hall of Fame in 2003. I felt honored to share the day with Eddie, as we had played one year together on the Dodgers and I truly respect his professional and yet passionate approach to baseball.

Giving my twenty minute speech at the Baseball Hall of Fame induction, I tried to thank all the people who had been there for me along the way— the managers, sportswriters, fans, and my family.

A photo with my family taken just moments after the Hall of Fame induction ceremony. (Back row: Kimmy; D.J.; Christy; her husband, Matt; front row: me and Sandy)

My brother-in-law, Jim Lahm, my good friend, Dave Mello (back row), and President Bush, with his grandson, Robert, at the HOF induction ceremony. President Bush is the only president to attend an induction ceremony.

The Expos celebrated a day in Montreal and Shea Stadium hosted "Gary Carter Night" after my induction into the Hall of Fame. It was an honor.

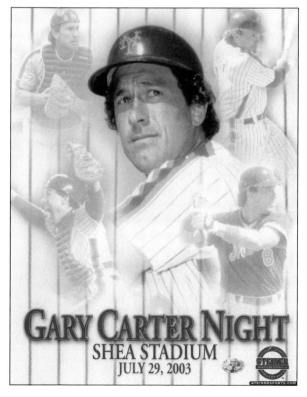

Managing the 2006 Championship Season in Port St. Lucie. Managing and working with young players has been something I've cherished since retiring from the major leagues.

Our family's 2007 Christmas photo. In the back row: Kyle, Kimmy's husband, and D.J.; middle row: Kimmy, me, and Matt; front row: Sandy, Christy, and our grandson, Carter James. Christy was pregnant when this photo was taken. The baby, Brady Matthew, was born on December 15, 2007.

he can literally go right into a computer room and look at his at-bat after it just happened. He can see how he was pitched to and try to figure out what he did wrong.

Is this for the better? In some ways it is, but to me they've taken the human element out of the game. It complicates things. Just go out and play the game!

I came from an era when players respected the game. You played hard, you hustled, and you employed a lot more strategy. You bunted guys over, you played hit and run, you used the squeeze play, and you tried to manufacture runs—all things that are pretty much a lost art today.

> *To me they've taken the human element out of the game. Just go out and play the game!*

In my day, baseball was more of a running game, especially in the National League. I don't think you're going to see another Rickey Henderson, Lou Brock, or Maury Wills. You're not going to see teams like the St. Louis Cardinals with their speed burners, Vince Coleman, Willie McGee, and Ozzie Smith.

When Jose Reyes of the Mets stole his 70th base late in the 2007 season, he was only the second player to steal as many as 70 bases since 2000. By comparison, in the decades of the '70s and '80s, some player stole at least 90 bases 11 times. That shows that the emphasis today is more on the home run. It has reverted to the style of Earl Weaver, the Baltimore Orioles manager who was ahead of his time. Weaver was unique in his day, the 1970s, abandoning little ball and stressing the three-run home run. Now everybody does it.

Today, the home-run hitter is king, and, again, it's because fans like home runs and go to games to see the big home-run hitters. People don't go to games to see a singles and doubles hitter. Take a guy like Craig Biggio, who's a throwback. He's played his whole career with one team, the Houston Astros. Because of free agency and interleague trading, you're not going to see many players like Ted Williams, Stan Musial, Mickey Mantle, Joe DiMaggio, Bob Gibson, Tony Gwynn, Johnny Bench, Cal Ripken Jr., George Brett, and Mike Schmidt, who played their entire major league careers with one team. Biggio has accumulated more than 3,000 hits, 89 percent of them singles and doubles. He's a Hall of Famer as far as I'm concerned, but nobody talks about him much. Why? Because he didn't hit a lot of home runs.

Television has been responsible for introducing the wild-card to baseball, for adding another tier to the playoffs, for expanding the League Championship series from a five-game series to seven, and for interleague play, all under the watch of Commissioner Bud Selig, and that's a feather in his cap. These changes were designed to increase fan interest and generate more revenue.

Because I'm a traditionalist, I was against those changes at first, but I have come to like them and to recognize that they have accomplished their goal. They have been good for baseball. The wild-card keeps more teams in the hunt for the playoffs and makes September games meaningful. Interleague play has sparked fan interest by pitting natural rivalries like the Yankees and Mets, the Cubs and White Sox, the Dodgers and Angels, the Giants and

Athletics against each other every year, and it has given fans of National League teams an opportunity to see in person the stars of the American League, and vice versa.

Despite all these sweeping changes in baseball over the past 20 years, one thing hasn't changed, and that's the game as it's played on the field. It's still 60 feet, six inches, from the pitcher to the batter and 90 feet between the bases. It's still nine innings, three outs to a side, four balls for a walk, three strikes and you're out. And it's still the greatest game ever created.

14

The Steroid Era

ON APRIL 8, 1974, MY 20TH BIRTHDAY, I WAS PLAYING FOR the Memphis Chicks, the Expos' Triple A farm team in the International League, when Henry Aaron hit his 715th home run off Al Downing of the Los Angeles Dodgers in Atlanta's Fulton County Stadium and passed the record of Babe Ruth.

It was a monumental milestone because of the perception everybody had of Babe Ruth. He was an icon, an idol recognized as the greatest baseball player of all time, and people thought his record would never be broken.

At the time, Barry Bonds was nine years old.

The first time I saw Barry was 12 years later, when he broke in as a rookie with the Pittsburgh Pirates and I was an established player, a 12-year major league veteran in my second season with the New York Mets. I saw a lot of Bonds as an opponent over the next six years, and I can remember what my impression was of him. He was listed in the press guide as 6'1" and 185 pounds, a lean, well-conditioned athlete but not a muscular brute. I saw him as a guy who was a five-tool player. He could run, throw, field, hit for average, and hit for power, but he was a hitter with holes in his swing. You could go up and in on him, and you could get him out with off-speed pitches. I thought he was a very good player who maybe had a chance to be a great player. But did I ever think that one day he was going to break Aaron's renowned career record of 755 home runs? No way.

> *But did I ever think that one day he was going to break Aaron's renowned career record of 755 home runs? No way.*

If you look at Barry Bonds today, he's not the same human being he was when I played against him. I know it's normal for people to get bigger as they get older, but not to the degree that Barry has. The size of his head and his neck, and the muscular development of his chest and arms, are enough to raise suspicions.

The steroid era probably began in the late 1980s, but it didn't reach the public's consciousness until 1993, the year after I retired, when guys who were never looked upon as power hitters began to put up big home-run numbers. In baseball's first 125 years, the 50-home-run mark was reached only 17 times, four of them by the incomparable Babe Ruth. Since 1995, the 50-homer plateau has been reached 23 times.

As discussed earlier, many things contributed to the rise in home runs, but the possibility of steroid use cannot be ignored. When I would walk into clubhouses at All-Star Games and look around at players, I would be amazed at how "ripped" some of them were, with bulging muscles; thick chests, biceps, and forearms; and veins on top of veins. It just didn't seem natural to me.

Suspicions arose in 1998 with the great home-run chase between Mark McGwire and Sammy Sosa, when McGwire hit 70 homers and Sosa belted 66 to storm past Roger Maris's single-season record of 61 set 37 years earlier. The following year, McGwire topped Sosa again, 65–63, and suspicions arose once again in 2001 when Bonds upped the single-season record to 73.

In the old days, 40 and 50 years ago, players never lifted weights. The belief back then was that being heavily muscled was counterproductive to playing baseball, which put a greater premium on flexibility rather than pure strength. Bat speed, not muscle, was what propelled baseballs great distances.

That started to change in the 1970s. In 1976, I broke my thumb. That winter I went on a Nautilus program, and I put on muscle. The next season, I hit 31 home runs, the second most I ever hit in any season. (The other year was 1985—I hit 32 with the Mets.)

By the late 1980s, every team had a personal trainer, and players began taking supplements and nutrients. Creatine, which helps put on muscle mass, became popular. All of it was legal.

The first indication of any wrongdoing was when a writer in St. Louis noticed that Mark McGwire had in his locker androstenedione, a steroid that builds muscle and had been banned by baseball. That opened a can of worms and got Commissioner Selig involved. Under Selig's direction, baseball instituted a testing program that the commissioner has claimed is the strongest and most thorough in sports. But the program calls for the testing of only about 10 percent of the players in the major leagues, so that really isn't much of a deterrent.

In his book, *Juiced*, Jose Canseco wrote of widespread steroid use in baseball and even pointed fingers and named names. That eventually led to Congress convening a panel to investigate the situation. The congressional hearings in 2005 served to give the problem widespread national attention when several of the game's biggest stars were summoned to Washington to testify before the committee.

Under oath, McGwire refused to answer questions about his steroid use and ducked the issue by saying, "I don't want to talk about the past. Let's talk about the future." Sosa, for his part, acted like he had difficulty with the English language, and Rafael Palmeiro pointed his finger and said, "I did not do steroids." A few weeks later, he failed a drug test.

The belief among baseball people is that Barry Bonds saw what McGwire and Sosa did and how much attention they got with their home-run chase, and he said to himself, "I'm the best player in the game. Why am I not getting the recognition I deserve?"

No charges ever have been brought against Bonds and in this country a person is innocent until proven guilty. But there is so much circumstantial evidence against him that the public's perception is that he must have used steroids.

It is believed that steroid use develops like this. First, a player starts spending a great deal of time in a gym, working out for hours at a time, multiple times a week. The next step is to ingest supplements to accelerate muscle growth and strength. But the legal supplements only get you so far, so the player turns to steroids. By his own admission, Bonds is a gym rat. He's always in the gym. I imagine the testosterone level created by the steroids is so high, it makes you want to go to the gym, and it's going to get you looking the way Barry does, with the bulging muscles and the enlarged head.

We have often heard apologists for Bonds, McGwire, and Sosa proclaim that steroids do not help a batter hit the ball. You still need excellent hand-eye coordination and bat speed. That's all true; however, there definitely is a correlation between the use of steroids and bat speed.

A recent study by a Tufts University physicist published in the *American Journal of Physics* said that steroids could help batters hit 50 percent more home runs by boosting their muscle mass by just 10 percent. The study says by putting on 10 percent more muscle mass, a batter can swing about 5 percent faster and increase the ball's speed by 4 percent as it leaves the bat.

The study says by putting on 10 percent more muscle mass, a batter can swing about 5 percent faster and increase the ball's speed by 4 percent as it leaves the bat.

"A 4 percent increase in ball speed, which can reasonably be expected from steroid use," writes the physicist, "can increase home-run production by anywhere from 50 percent to 100 percent. An extra 10 pounds of muscle can add just enough extra to a batter's swing to send the ball out of the park." The bottom line is that the use of steroids is not only illegal, it's cheating.

The most incriminating evidence against Bonds is how his home-run totals have escalated as he got older. At an age when most players are on the decline, Barry got better. In his first seven seasons, Bonds hit 176 home runs, an average of 25.1 per season. In his next 12 years, he hit 527 homers, an average of 43.9 per season. It's unheard of. It defies reason. What's even more amazing is at age 37, he broke the single season record for home runs with 73.

At the age of 38, my career was over. Look at what Bonds has done since he turned 38—46 home runs in the year of his 38th birthday, 45 home runs in the year of his 39th birthday, and 45 home runs in the year of his 40th birthday. Even at that advanced age, he continued to be the most feared hitter in baseball, and opponents avoided pitching to him. In those three seasons, he drew 198, 148, and the staggering total of 232 walks and 120 intentional walks.

Unfortunately, there are many athletes who are willing to risk those dangers, or even trade several years of their life for the benefits steroid use provides.

There's no doubt in my mind, if I had taken steroids I could have extended my career by three or four years. Would I have taken steroids if they were available in my day? The temptation would have been great, I admit, but I like to think I would have had enough self-control to resist that temptation, especially after what we have learned about the harmful side effects of taking steroids. Unfortunately, there are many athletes who are willing to risk those dangers, or even trade several years of their life for the benefits steroid use provides.

Again, that's another example of how the game is money-driven. Players take steroids to improve their performance and lengthen their careers, which in turn leads to bigger contracts for a longer period of time.

Another factor is ego and competitiveness. A professional athlete is, by nature, a competitor. He strives to be the best at what he does. If he sees others improving their performance and getting recognition, it's only natural that he would want to do what it takes to keep up with the competition.

One of the biggest stories from the 2007 baseball season was the emergence of Rick Ankiel of the St. Louis Cardinals as a home-run hitter. Ankiel had been a highly touted prospect as a pitcher in the mid-nineties, a "can't miss" pitcher who could throw the ball. He won 11 games in the 2000 season and then all of a sudden he couldn't throw the ball over the plate. In one playoff game against the Braves, he unleashed five wild pitches in two and two-thirds innings. It was mysterious.

When Ankiel continued to have trouble with his control the following spring, the Cardinals sent him to the minor leagues, where his control problems continued. Ultimately, Ankiel gave up pitching and decided to try a comeback as an outfielder. In 2007, he hit 32 home runs for Memphis of the Pacific Coast League and was recalled by the Cardinals in August.

With the Cardinals, Ankiel hit three home runs in his first three games, nine in his first 80 at-bats. He was being compared with two baseball legends, Babe Ruth and Stan Musial, both of whom gave up pitching and became Hall of Fame hitters. It was a heartwarming story, the feel-good story of the summer. Ankiel had reinvented himself. His perseverance and determination brought admiration and were awe-inspiring.

Everybody is under suspicion, the innocent as well as the guilty.

And then Ankiel's bubble burst when it was revealed that he had taken human growth hormones. He presumably did so at a time when HGH had not been banned by baseball, but the damage was done. Cynics would not embrace the idea that Ankiel had accomplished what he had without the aid of illegal substances. He remains under suspicion, as do Troy Glaus, who also was accused of using HGH, and Bonds, Sosa, and McGwire.

Unfortunately, the scourge of steroids and HGH has tarnished the game of baseball. Everybody is under suspicion, the innocent as well as the guilty. Records are tainted. If a player breaks a home-run record or merely increases his home-run production from one year to the next, he's immediately suspected of cheating. That player may be innocent, but if the public perception is that he's guilty, that's just as harmful to the game and to that player as if he had failed a drug test.

15

The Best I've Seen

MY OLD MONTREAL EXPOS MANAGER GENE MAUCH once was quoted as saying that he believed the decades of the '60s and '70s produced more great baseball players than any other two decades in history.

Who am I to question the opinion of a man whom many have called one of the great baseball minds? So I'll accept Mauch's opinion and consider it a compliment since the first five years of my career came in the '70s. And from my experience and observation, I'd have to say that Mauch's opinion is right on.

Just look at the players who competed in the 1970s and made the Hall of Fame: Gaylord Perry, Nolan Ryan, Bruce Sutter, Bob Gibson, Jim Palmer, Tom Seaver, Catfish Hunter, Hoyt Wilhelm, Rollie Fingers, Don Sutton, Jim Bunning, Juan Marichal, Dennis Eckersley, Ferguson Jenkins, Steve Carlton, Phil Niekro.

Also Johnny Bench, Carlton Fisk, Willie McCovey, Orlando Cepeda, Eddie Murray, Tony Perez, Harmon Killebrew, Rod Carew, Joe Morgan, George Brett, Mike

Schmidt, Paul Molitor, Brooks Robinson, Ernie Banks, Robin Yount, Luis Aparicio.

As well as Ozzie Smith, Carl Yastrzemski, Willie Stargell, Lou Brock, Billy Williams, Willie Mays, Al Kaline, Henry Aaron, Reggie Jackson, Frank Robinson, Roberto Clemente, and Dave Winfield.

Wow!

> *I played with so many great players.*

Many of those players I never played against or even saw because when I arrived in the major leagues to stay in 1975, some of them had already retired, and there was no inter-league play back then, so I didn't get to see the American Leaguers except in spring training. I will therefore confine my discussion here to the greatest players I played with or against.

The best player I played with for a length of time was Andre Dawson, who was my teammate in Montreal for eight seasons. With all due respect to all my other team-mates, if I had to pick one, it would be "Hawk." He was a true professional, which is the greatest compliment one player can give to another.

Another true professional was the guy who went into the Hall of Fame the same time I did, Eddie Murray. But I played with him for only one year, with the Dodgers in 1991.

I played with so many great players. Tim Raines was one. So was Ellis Valentine, a tremendous player whom I thought was going to have a great career, but he had some off-field issues. The same goes for Darryl Strawberry. Both Valentine and Strawberry had unbelievable natural ability and should have had greater careers than they did, but their problems off the field prevented them from reaching their full potential.

I don't want to take anything away from Eddie Murray, but the best first baseman I ever played with as far as fielding and clutch hitting was Keith Hernandez.

I caught a lot of great pitchers in All-Star Games, but among the pitchers I caught regularly, the best for one season was Dwight "Doc" Gooden in 1985. He went 24–4 with a 1.53 ERA, 268 strikeouts, and eight shutouts, and he won the Cy Young Award—all at the age of 20. Doc, too, had off-field issues that prevented him from having what could have been a Hall of Fame career.

Steve Rogers was the Expos' best pitcher in the years I was there, the ace of the staff. He won 158 games in 13 years. In Montreal, I caught other excellent pitchers like Bill Gullickson, Scott Sanderson, and David Palmer. (Randy Johnson left Montreal three years before I returned there, and Pedro Martinez came along two years after I retired.)

And then there was Charlie Lea, who pitched a no-hitter in 1981. Lea was a blond-haired kid, about 6'4", who came from Memphis, Tennessee, but was born in Orleans, France (his father was a career army man), which came in handy when he played in French-speaking Montreal.

Charlie pitched his no-hitter against the Giants in the second game of a doubleheader. I caught both games, and I remember Billy Norton made the last out of Lea's no-hitter. I caught some one-hitters, but that was the only no-hitter I ever caught in more than 2,000 major league games behind the plate. I didn't catch a no-hitter with the Mets because, hard to believe, no Mets pitcher has ever thrown a no-hitter in their almost 50-year history.

Lea looked like he was going to be a tremendous pitcher for a long time for the Expos. He won 16 games in 1983 and was the starting and winning pitcher for the National League in the 1984 All-Star Game in San Francisco. That season, he won 15 games, but soon afterward he developed arm problems that cut short his career. He never won another game for the Expos. He tried a comeback and pitched one year for the Twins, finishing his career with a record of 62–48.

It's also another example of why professional athletes must plan for the future because they never know when their careers will be cut short.

The sad story of Charlie Lea is one more example of a career that was ended prematurely, another reason professional athletes should not be criticized for getting as much money as they can when they have the chance. It's also another example of why professional athletes must plan for the future because they never know when their careers will be cut short.

In New York, I had the pleasure of catching that excellent Mets staff in 1986, with Gooden, Ron Darling, Sid Fernandez, Bobby Ojeda, and Rick Aguilera. Later with the Mets I caught David Cone, who had a season in 1988 that came close to Gooden's 1985 season. Coney and I really clicked. That year he was 20–3 with a 2.22 earned-run average, four shutouts, and 213 strikeouts, and he finished second to Orel Hershiser in the Cy Young Award voting.

With the Giants, I caught a veteran staff that included Mike LaCoss, Kelly Downs, Atlee Hammaker, and Scott Garrelts, guys who were not considered great pitchers, but they were a pleasure to catch. Also on that team was Rick Reuschel, who had been a 20-game winner with the Cubs and was near the end of his career. I couldn't figure out how he got hitters out with the stuff he threw up there, but he did. By then he was no longer overpowering, but he knew how to pitch. He'd throw a little slider, a little sinker, a little curveball—nothing spectacular, but he got hitters out.

In 1991 with the Dodgers I caught Orel Hershiser, but he was coming back from rotator cuff surgery and he was not the same pitcher he had been when he won the Cy Young Award and broke the record for consecutive scoreless innings in 1988.

Among the great relief pitchers I caught are Jeff Reardon, Jesse Orosco, Roger McDowell, Jeff Brantley, Steve Bedrosian, and Jay Howell.

One of the questions I am asked most frequently is: who was the toughest pitcher you faced?

If you want to go strictly by the numbers, the pitcher who gave me the most trouble was a guy even the most ardent baseball fans probably never heard of. His name is Mark Lee, and he pitched for San Diego and Pittsburgh from 1978 to 1981. He won only seven games in his major league career. I batted against him seven times and didn't get a hit. There are many pitchers who held me hitless in my career, but none for more than seven at-bats.

Against pitchers I faced more often, the one who comes to mind that was the toughest for me was Don Robinson,

Against pitchers I faced more often, the one who comes to mind that was the toughest for me was Don Robinson...

a right-hander with the Pirates and later the Giants. My career numbers against him were 9-for-57, a .158 average, with three doubles, one home run, and eight RBIs. But most of my hits off him came late in his career. When he was with the Pirates, I probably hit under .100 against him. When he went to the Giants, I hit him a little better. I got my 300th double and my 1,000th RBI against him.

In my career, I batted against a lot of great pitchers, including 11 who are in the Hall of Fame and many more, like Greg Maddux, Tom Glavine, Jim Kaat, Tommy John, Bert Blyleven, John Smoltz, Lee Smith, and Curt Schilling, who someday will be in the Hall of Fame or who have come close to being elected.

I should point out that in some cases, I hit against these pitchers when they were young and hadn't yet reached their peak, or when they were on the downside of their careers.

Having said that, early in my career, around 1975, the pitcher I thought was the best was Tom Seaver. I did some research and found that in my career I was 12-for-64 against Seaver, an average of .188, with one home run, four RBIs, and 12 strikeouts.

The thing about Tom is that I never felt overwhelmed against him. He was just a good pitcher who threw hard, had a great slider, and showed pinpoint control. When hitters of my era talk about a pitcher who was over-whelming, they invariably mention J.R. Richard of the

Houston Astros, who was overpowering before he suffered a stroke. They weren't using radar guns back in the day, but I'm convinced Richard threw 100 miles per hour. Nevertheless, I never felt intimidated by him, and I hit him well. I got my first grand slam against him, and my career numbers against Richard were 14-for-39, a .359 average, with three home runs and 11 RBIs.

Nolan Ryan is another guy who overpowered hitters. Early in my career, Nolan was pitching in the American League, and I didn't get to face him. The first time I saw him in person was when he started for the American League in the 1979 All-Star Game. (Unfortunately, I didn't start the game and Ryan was out of the game when I got in.) Davey Lopes was the first batter for the National League. Ryan struck Lopes out, and Davey came back to the bench and said, "Ohhh my God, guys, be ready. He has turned it up a notch."

Ryan was throwing so hard you could hear it from the dugout, "Whooshhh!"

As overpowering as Nolan was, when I finally faced him I never felt intimidated by him. The way I approached him was to sit on pitches. When he was behind in the count, I would sit on his breaking ball. I figured out that he would try to fool you with his breaking ball because he could throw it for strikes and then if he got ahead, he'd try to put you away with his fastball. But if he got behind in the count, he'd throw his breaking ball, and that's what I was sitting on.

As overpowering as Nolan was, when I finally faced him I never felt intimidated by him.

As a result, I did pretty well against him. In 49 at-bats against Ryan, I had 13 hits for a .265 average with three doubles, two home runs, nine RBIs, and seven strikeouts.

I mentioned that I faced 11 Hall of Fame pitchers in my career, and I have told you how I fared against two of them, Tom Seaver and Nolan Ryan. Because I looked it up, I can pass along my numbers against the other nine. I'll list them alphabetically and without comment, except to say that I respected every one of them.

PITCHER	MY CAREER STATS AGAINST	AVERAGE	HOME RUNS	RBIS
Steve Carlton	36-for-116	.310	11	24
Dennis Eckersley	7-for-29	.241	2	4
Rollie Fingers	2-for-11	.182	0	0
Bob Gibson	2-for-4	.500	0	1
Ferguson Jenkins	7-for-13	.538	1	2
Phil Niekro	8-for-43	.186	3	5
Gaylord Perry	4-for-11	.364	1	5
Bruce Sutter	16-for-45	.356	3	11
Don Sutton	14-for-54	.259	1	4

To a certain degree, being a catcher helps you as a hitter. A catcher learns to think along with a pitcher, and you get a feel for how he wants to get hitters out, so all my years of catching helped me figure out how a pitcher was going to work on me.

I wasn't a "guess" hitter who would go up to bat and try to figure out what the pitcher was going to throw in certain counts. I was more of a "location" hitter. I would look for a pitch in a specific location. I liked the ball from the middle of the plate in. That was my "happy zone" and if you threw it there,

To a certain degree, being a catcher helps you as a hitter.

I wasn't going to miss it. If you made that mistake, I was going to do some damage.

The book on me was to throw me hard stuff up and in and breaking stuff low and away, but you can say the same thing about most hitters. As time went on, I did better against pitchers I faced more often than pitchers I was facing for the first time, and that's also common.

In my opinion, the best pitch in baseball, and the toughest pitch for a catcher to catch, is the backup slider. It's a pitch that when thrown by a right-handed pitcher is meant to break away from a right-handed hitter, but instead it breaks into a right-handed hitter. It's unintentional, but it's very effective. I still hold the record for catchers by having only one passed ball in a season in which I caught more than 150 games, but when I did get passed balls, they usually were on the backup slider.

In my opinion, the best pitch in baseball, and the toughest pitch for a catcher to catch, is the backup slider.

Being a catcher helps you with the thought process between pitcher and hitter and could make you a better hitter, but the wear and tear of catching runs you down and weakens you. That's why there have been only two National League catchers who have won batting titles. Bubbles Hargrave of Cincinnati won it way back in 1926, and Ernie Lombardi won it twice, for Cincinnati in 1938 and for Boston in 1942. Then it took 64 years for another catcher to win a batting title when, in 2006, Joe Mauer of the Minnesota Twins batted .347 and became the first catcher in the American League to win the batting championship. As someone who caught more than 2,000 games; took foul tips off the hands, the chest, the shoulders; went into a crouch hundreds of thousands of times; and had all kinds of injuries and more than a dozen operations, I find that amazing.

Mauer is one of a small group of good catchers playing today. I admire Mike Piazza for his great hitting. He turned himself into a great and tremendously productive hitter. He's hit more home runs as a catcher than anybody else in history, and he has a lifetime batting average over .300. In 1997, he even vied for a batting title. He hit .362 for the Dodgers, third in the National League behind Tony Gwynn and Larry Walker. That's phenomenal. I can't even comprehend that. My highest average was .294 in one season.

Another active catcher I like is Pudge Rodriguez, without a doubt. He's an excellent receiver and catch-and-throw guy, and he's proven himself hitting. He broke Bench's record for Gold Gloves when he won his 11th in 2004. Early in his career, in Texas, he had a knock against him that he didn't call a good game, but he has put that behind him by winning a World Series with the Marlins and helping to bring along the young pitchers with the Tigers. Pudge is the modern-day standard for catchers.

I like Brad Ausmus, a good catch-and-throw guy, and Jorge Posada, who seems to get better as he gets older. He had his best offensive season at the age of 36 and is piling up some very good numbers.

I have been impressed with what I have seen of the Dodgers' young catcher, Russell Martin, and the Braves' Brian McCann, especially as a hitter, but there aren't a lot of good catchers today, especially young ones.

When I first came up, they told me, "We're not so concerned about your bat as we are about your defense." But you don't get consideration for the Hall of Fame only for your catching. You have to hit, too. Look at the ones who are in the Hall of Fame: all good hitters.

And that's why when it comes to catchers, number one in my book is Johnny Bench, who many veteran baseball observers say is the greatest catcher ever. Not only was he a great defensive catcher who won 10 Gold Gloves, but he was also a big run producer. John is the best I ever saw. I'll put in my disclaimer here and repeat that I obviously never saw the great catchers of the past: Roger Bresnahan, Mickey Cochrane, Gabby Hartnett, Bill Dickey, Yogi Berra, and Roy Campanella. But I can't imagine any of them being better than Bench.

> *And that's why when it comes to catchers, number one in my book is Johnny Bench, who many veteran baseball observers say is the greatest catcher ever.*

Johnny definitely was the guy back in 1972 when I first signed with the Expos. When I became a catcher, he was the one I wanted to emulate. He developed the one-handed style of catching, and I'm indebted to him for that because I adopted that style; as a result my fingers are pretty straight, considering all the catching I did.

I took a few foul tips as all catchers do, but for the most part I was always very conscientious about protecting my throwing hand. I learned that from Bench. Whenever there was a runner on base, I would tuck my thumb and put my bare hand behind the glove. Therefore, for the most part, I was able to avoid taking foul tips on my hand.

I remember seeing a foul tip split John Stearns's finger, and he was never the same after that.

Besides Bench, I liked the way Jerry Grote received. I thought Steve Yeager was a good catch-and-throw guy, and so was Bob Boone. Ted Simmons rates high, especially as a hitter.

Carlton Fisk came along about the same time I did. He got a lot of recognition as a catcher and deservedly so. I heard a lot about Thurman Munson, but I can't remember ever playing against him or even having the chance to talk to him. I would have remembered that. I hear he was a tough competitor, a gamer, and a hard-nosed player, my kind of guy. So I'm sure I would have liked him for that. They say he didn't have a great arm but that he had a quick release. Playing my entire career in the National League, I regret not getting a chance to see, and compete against, guys like Fisk and Munson.

But in my era, it was Johnny Bench.

16

Looking Ahead

AS I LOOK AT BASEBALL TODAY AS A FAN—I STILL FOLLOW the game very closely—and I see all the great young players coming along and making their mark, I am convinced that the game of baseball is in very good hands. I am amazed at the size, strength, and speed of today's players. Baseball's future is very bright.

Speaking as someone who has had experience managing in the low minor leagues, in the Instructional League, and in the Futures Game, what I look for in young players—and I'm old school about this—is whether they have a love and passion for the game. When I broke into professional baseball, I lacked a lot of the fundamentals and technique as a catcher, a position I had never played. But my coaches could see my love, passion, and enthusiasm for the game. I loved to play. I even loved to practice.

I am convinced that the game of baseball is in very good hands.

How a player handles the game and respects the game tells me more about a young guy than merely his ability, although ability certainly is important. For example, if a young player doesn't hustle, it tells me he doesn't have the desire, no matter how talented he is. And if he doesn't have the desire or enthusiasm or passion for the game, he's not going to improve and he's probably not going to make it.

But if he comes to the ballpark on time, is willing to learn, is willing to go into the batting cage and work on his hitting; or if a catcher is willing to put in the time to work on blocking balls, catching balls, and throwing to second base; or if an infielder is willing to take hundreds of ground balls every day, those kinds of things—the will to learn and to improve—will tell me a great deal about that kid. That player, if he does all those things, has a chance.

I truly believe the kids I managed learned a lot from me. I tried to make sure they always knew where I was coming from. First, I let them know I cared about them. Second, the one thing I insisted on was that they play hard. If they didn't play hard, they would get the full extent of my wrath, but once I had let them have it, I would make sure to give them a pat on the back to let them know I cared.

Toward the end of the 2006 season at Port St. Lucie in the Florida State League I was sent a 17-year-old out-fielder named Fernando Martinez, who has a world of ability and who the Mets regard as one of their top prospects. They had signed him as a 16-year-old for a bonus of $1.4 million. When I got Martinez, my instructions were to play him every day in center field. However, he was hitting under .200, and there were a couple of times that he would hit a pop-up and not run hard to first base, so I benched him.

You can bet I got a call from the front office asking why I benched Martinez.

"I'm trying to teach the kid a lesson," I said.

"Okay," I was told, "but he's in there tomorrow, right?"

I put him back in the lineup, and, guess what, he hustled after that. I never had another problem with him.

In the Gulf Coast Rookie League in 2005, I had a Canadian kid named Emanuel Garcia, an infielder. When I watched him take batting practice, this kid couldn't hit the ball out of the infield. He was getting jammed constantly. Defensively, he couldn't throw the ball accurately, and he wasn't very sure-handed on ground balls. When I first saw him, I said to myself there's no way this kid is going to make it. The ball was knocking the bat out of his hands.

That's the kind of kid who will catch my attention. He had the desire to get better and a great work ethic.

But he worked very hard. He had a passion for the game, and he was willing to put in the time to improve. He took extra batting practice. He worked on his throws. He took extra ground balls. And if he made a mistake, he was hard on himself. This kid wound up hitting over .300 for me and won the Sterling Mets award as the Most Valuable Player on my team.

That's the kind of kid who will catch my attention. He had the desire to get better and a great work ethic. He went from being a player who I thought had no chance of making it to being one who has a chance. If he doesn't make it, it will be because of a lack of ability, not a lack of effort.

If I were a scout and I looked at a high school kid, I would want to see what kind of arm he has, what kind of bat he has, how he maneuvers the ball, whether he hits it to all fields, whether he hustles. Simply, how does he play the game? If he shows you all those things, then you can develop him. But if you see a kid who is lackadaisical and doesn't hustle, doesn't run balls out, and has an attitude, then I would say forget about it. If he's showing those things in high school, he's probably going to show those same things as a professional.

I wanted to play up to the potential of what I was earning. That was my incentive.

Baseball is a team game, yet you are rewarded based on what you do individually. When I played, I always wanted to live up to the rewards I got contractually and the expectations that came with those rewards. If I was going to be paid a certain amount of money—and the amount didn't matter—I wanted to earn it. I wanted to play up to the potential of what I was earning. That was my incentive.

When it comes to young pitchers, I believe there's an overemphasis these days on the ability to throw hard. If you go to a high school or college game, you'll see the scouts all with their radar guns clocking how hard a kid is throwing, and if that kid is not getting it up there in the mid-90s, the scouts will rule him out as a prospect.

Jamie Moyer, for example, would never be signed today. He can't break a pane of glass, but he's won more than 200 major league games because he knows how to pitch.

Greg Maddux is another one. When he first came up with the Cubs and I faced him, I looked at this scrawny little kid out there, maybe 6' tall, but I doubt it, and about 170 pounds. He had good stuff and an assortment of pitches, but he didn't blow you away. I never thought he would be a 300-game winner. He might have thrown in the low 90s when he was young, but for the past 10 years, he has topped out at 86–88 miles per hour.

Maddux made himself into an outstanding pitcher because he learned how to pitch. He learned to pitch with his God-given ability, and he got movement on his ball, which does not show up on a radar gun but is more important than speed for getting hitters out.

The Mets had a young minor league pitcher, who moved on to the Marlins organization last season, named Blake McGinley, who has never been regarded as a prospect. He can't break 90 miles per hour, but he gets hitters out and he has always had a low ERA. He may be one of those guys about whom they say he'll be a nonprospect all the way to the major leagues.

What I'm saying is that if I were scouting a high school pitcher I wouldn't eliminate him because he doesn't throw hard. I would look at how he is as a competitor and whether he knows how to pitch, and I would give him the benefit of the doubt. I wouldn't erase him just because he doesn't throw in the mid-90s. But today most scouts go only by their radar gun. They want guys who throw in the mid-90s, and if you don't throw over 90, they won't give you a second look.

I would look at how he is as a competitor and whether he knows how to pitch, and I would give him the benefit of the doubt.

Some organizations will rule out a pitcher if he isn't at least 6'4". Does that mean guys like Maddux and Moyer, Ron Guidry and Whitey Ford wouldn't even get a tumble today? Huston Street and Tim Hudson are both barely 6' and some teams probably wouldn't even look at them.

Another of my pet peeves is the pitch count, something that has crept into the game in the past 15 or 20 years. I'm not an advocate for pitch counts, but it has become so prominent in today's game with every organization. Maybe they're trying to protect pitchers, but I can't understand where that protection comes in when you consider that all the great pitchers of the past never were on pitch counts.

Jim Kaat, a man whose opinions on pitching I respect enormously, was never on a pitch count, and he pitched in the major leagues for 25 years, appeared in 898 games, won 283, and never had arm problems. "Kitty" used to throw every day, in a game or on the side, because he believes, and I agree, that the arm is a muscle and a muscle will rust out before it wears out.

One season Kaat pitched 19 complete games. Today, you won't have 19 complete games in a season from all the major league teams combined.

Go back further. Robin Roberts, who won 286 games and is in the Hall of Fame, once pitched 28 consecutive complete games. I don't think he was ever on a pitch count.

The pitch count is one of the main reasons you don't see many complete games these days. Pitchers are conditioned to throw a minimum of pitches from the time they're in Little League, which is a good thing. When a kid is 10, 11, 12 years old, he shouldn't throw a lot of pitches because his arm isn't fully developed. Throwing a baseball as hard as you can is an unnatural arm action, and kids can hurt their arms throwing too much.

On the other hand, the only way to gain arm strength is to throw, so there's a dilemma. But coaches have a tendency to err on the side of caution, and so the pitch count has become prevalent. Today, they limit the number of pitches not only in Little League, but also in high school, in college, in the minor leagues, and even in the majors.

When I was managing in the Rookie League, I was under orders to limit my pitchers to about 50 pitches in their first start and then gradually build them up to 65 pitches and then to 75, which was the maximum. Even in the major leagues, when a starting pitcher is getting close to 100 pitches, it seems a caution sign goes off in the manager's head, and the bullpen starts cranking. And it doesn't matter how effective the starter was.

Because they have been conditioned all through their careers to limit the number of pitches, major league starters will reach a pitch count of 100, start feeling fatigue, and begin thinking maybe it's time to come out.

One of the biggest changes in baseball on the field over the past 20 or 30 years has been the emergence of the relief pitcher, or closer, as a position of prominence. In many ways, the closer has become more valuable than the starter because he can influence the outcome of anywhere from 40 to 60 games a season, while the starter can influence the outcome of only 25 or 30 games.

Baseball, at least the pitching part of it, has become a game of specialists. If a manager has a staff of starters who can go six or seven strong innings consistently, he's going to be very successful because he won't deplete his bullpen. Guys are going to be fresh.

Baseball, at least the pitching part of it, has become a game of specialists.

Here again money comes into the picture. If a team is paying a closer like Mariano Rivera $10 million a year to come in to pitch to one hitter or for one inning to save a game, they're going to use him. That's how today's game is scripted. You give it to your starter, and then you turn it over to your setup guy and then to your closer. Most teams even designate a pitcher as a seventh-inning guy, an eighth-inning guy, and a closer. The starter could be lights-out, not allow a run for seven innings, and he'll still be removed. Regardless of how dominant the starter has been, if a manager doesn't bring in his closer, he's certain to hear about it from his owner or general manager. "Why are we paying this closer $10 million a year if you're not going to use him?"

The reason teams are overprotective of their players, especially pitchers, is that they have a huge financial investment in players. Toward that end, in recent years baseball has done a tremendous job in promoting and showcasing its young talent. They have done this in several ways. In 2007, for the first time, the free-agent draft was televised nationally. It's still not as big a deal as the pro football and pro basketball drafts, but it does give baseball fans an opportunity to learn the names of the top prospects from high school and college, the future stars of the game, and to follow their progress up the minor league ladder.

In recent years baseball has done a tremendous job in promoting and showcasing its young talent.

Another way baseball showcases its young talent is with the Futures Game, which is part of the three-day major league All-Star Game festivities. It matches two teams of top minor league prospects, one made up of players from the United States, the other of players who come from outside the United States. In 2006, I had the honor of managing the U.S. team (Ferguson Jenkins managed the World team). On my team I had such promising players as Hunter Pence, Howie Kendrick, Phil Hughes, Billy Butler, Alex Gordon, Ryan Braun, and Stephen Drew. It was a great thrill for me to manage that team and to see those prospects come along. Since I managed them and got to know them, I have continued to follow them. They're all in the major leagues now and doing very well.

Look around at every team in baseball, and you'll see young players like Hanley Ramirez, Jose Reyes, Joe Mauer, David Wright, B.J. Upton, Joba Chamberlain, Dustin Pedroia, James Loney, Prince Fielder, Ryan Braun, and many others who are the stars of the future.

Players are getting bigger, faster, stronger, and better. And that's why I say baseball is in good hands and why I am optimistic about the future of the game.

17

Future Hall of Famers

IN CASE THEY HAVEN'T CONSIDERED IT ALREADY, AND they probably have, here's a word of caution for the good people at the Baseball Hall of Fame in Cooperstown, New York: you had better prepare for expansion because looking down the road, I see an explosion coming.

In the next 25 years or so, the number of players in the Hall of Fame (currently 198 with the election of Cal Ripken Jr. and Tony Gwynn; there are also 35 players from the Negro Leagues, 16 managers, eight umpires, and 23 executives) is probably going to double.

Let me start by discussing five controversial figures, Barry Bonds, Mark McGwire, Sammy Sosa, Rafael Palmeiro, and Pete Rose, all of whom probably would be certain Hall of Famers were it not for the suspicion surrounding their performances and/or the charges brought against them.

My feeling about those five players is slightly contrary to what other Hall of Famers feel, particularly the elder statesmen, like Bob Feller. Feller is the senior living member of the Hall of Fame in terms of the number of years he's been in (he was inducted in 1962), and Bob has been very vocal and very adamant against those five players because he did everything naturally.

I appreciate the fact that he played in an era when there was no such thing as steroids and HGH and that he gave up almost four full seasons to serve his country as a navy gun captain during World War II, earning five campaign ribbons and eight battle stars, and yet he had a phenomenal career—266 wins, 2,581 strikeouts, three no-hitters, and 12 one-hitters. The career he had was unbelievable.

I kind of go along with the elder statesmen in one sense: we must ask, are these five players deserving of a place in Cooperstown?

Take Pete Rose, whose situation is different from the other four. He's in a category similar to "Shoeless" Joe Jackson, who has the third highest lifetime batting average in baseball history, .356. Jackson was banned from baseball for allegedly conspiring to fix the 1919 World Series and is not in the Hall of Fame, even though he was acquitted in a court of law.

I admire Pete Rose tremendously.

I admire Pete Rose tremendously. I tried to emulate him as a player because of his all-out hustle, his reputation as "Charlie Hustle." And yet there is so much opposition to him because of what he did, betting on baseball games, and because he has shown no remorse for his deeds.

For years he refused to admit he bet on baseball. Then, 14 years after he became eligible for the Hall of Fame and with only one year of eligibility left on the Baseball Writers ballot, he told television host Charlie Rose (no relation to Pete), "Yes, I did bet on baseball," after denying it all those years. That just puts a black mark on the game.

As anyone who has spent any time in a professional clubhouse or dugout knows, the number-one rule in baseball, the one thing that won't be tolerated, is betting on the game. It's the most egregious sin a player can commit, greater than any other crime, including the use of performance-enhancing drugs. The "No Betting" sign is in every professional clubhouse and every professional dugout.

My suggestion where Rose is concerned is a compromise. Acknowledge and recognize him as the all-time hits leader with a commemorative plaque, but don't give him his day in Cooperstown by formally electing him to the Hall of Fame.

The other four are a different kettle of fish. Take Bonds. In my opinion, he already was a Hall of Famer, one of the greatest players the game has known, before the steroid scandal hit. His record for the most home runs in a season and in a career, his phenomenal .609 on-base percentage and 232 walks in 2004, and his seven Most Valuable Player awards cannot be denied, with or without steroids.

Take Bonds. In my opinion, he already was a Hall of Famer, one of the greatest players the game has known, before the steroid scandal hit.

The only thing that could keep Bonds out of the Hall of Fame would be if Major League Baseball provided proof that he was a steroid user and his name was kept off the ballot. Were it not for the steroid thing, Barry might have been the first unanimous selection for the Hall of Fame, or, at least, he might have received the highest percentage of votes ever. Instead, I expect him to fall far short of that, but I think he'll easily get the 75 percent of the vote that is required for election.

Despite his 70 home runs in 1998 and his 583 career home runs, I'm not sure Mark McGwire had a Hall of Fame career because he was such a one-dimensional player. He wasn't a five-tool player. He wasn't a particularly good fielder. He couldn't run (only six triples and 12 stolen bases in 14 seasons), and he didn't hit for a high average (lifetime .263). He was a home-run hitter, that's it. That might have been enough to get him elected, but in his first year of eligibility he received only 23 percent of the vote from the Baseball Writers, which was obviously a backlash against his suspected steroid use.

Sammy Sosa, with more than 600 home runs in his career, is in the same category. If McGwire isn't elected, there's no way Sammy will be.

If McGwire isn't elected, there's no way Sammy will be.

Palmeiro's denial at the congressional hearings and his subsequent exposure as a steroid user will follow him for the rest of his days. He will be remembered more for that than for what he accomplished on the baseball field, and here's a guy who joined an elite group with Henry Aaron, Willie Mays, and Eddie Murray, all Hall of Famers, as the only players in baseball history to hit 500 homers and get 3,000 hits. Those numbers normally would make Palmeiro a certainty for the Hall of Fame, but his eligibility is coming up and the voters are going to forget the 500 home runs and 3,000 hits and instead remember what he told Congress and that he got caught.

Of the retired players who still are not in the Hall of Fame, I'm baffled that Andre Dawson, Jim Rice, Bert Blyleven, and Jack Morris have not been elected.

Dawson, "the Hawk," my teammate in Montreal, deserves to be elected. He has more than 2,700 hits, more than 1,500 RBIs, and more than 400 home runs, and he won the MVP in 1987 with a last-place team, the Cubs. And he joined that elite group with Willie Mays, Barry Bonds, Bobby Bonds, Reggie Sanders, and Steve Finley as the only players with 300 home runs and 300 stolen bases. Because I played with him and saw him regularly, I put Dawson ahead of Rice, who was not as good defensively and didn't run as well as Hawk.

I didn't see much of Rice, but I know he put up some powerful numbers in a 14-year span. I think Jim belongs. He was the dominant power hitter of his time with eight seasons of 100 or more RBIs and seven seasons over .300.

I don't look at Rice as being as complete a player as Andre, yet Jim has received more Hall of Fame votes than Dawson. Why? The only thing I can think of is that Hawk played all those years in Montreal.

I can't understand what the voters have against Blyleven, who won 287 games as a pitcher and was third of all time in strikeouts when he retired. He was nasty. He had the best right-handed curveball in the game when I was playing.

Morris has 254 wins and a reputation as a big-game pitcher, 3–2 in League Championship Series, 4–2 in the World Series.

Among those who have not yet appeared on the ballot, I believe Rickey Henderson, the greatest base stealer and greatest leadoff hitter ever, will make it, as will Roberto Alomar. And Jeff Bagwell should get some support.

Among active players, there are about two dozen who I believe will be elected to the Hall of Fame and another dozen or so who are on the fence.

There was a time when 500 home runs was an automatic ticket to Cooperstown, but the home run has become so cheap these days, we may be reaching a point where 500 home runs may not get you elected. We have already seen the backlash against McGwire with his 583 home runs and we're probably going to see the same thing when Sosa is eligible. But what about Jim Thome and Frank Thomas, who have joined the 500-home-run club, and Manny Ramirez and Gary Sheffield, who are about to?

Ramirez, to me, is a no-brainer, but Thome, Thomas, and Sheffield may have a tough time getting the necessary 75 percent.

Frank Thomas, "the Big Hurt," is an interesting case. He's obviously a great hitter, with a .300 career average, more than 1,600 RBIs, 11 seasons with 100 or more RBIs, 10 seasons hitting over .300, and two MVP awards, but he spent the majority of his career as a designated hitter, which brings up another question. How are the voters going to regard guys who spent their careers as designated hitters, like Edgar Martinez, with a .312 career batting average, and David "Big Papi" Ortiz, the game's most dangerous clutch hitter?

Do you keep them out of the Hall of Fame because they didn't play defense? There are players in the Hall of Fame, such as Ted Williams and Ralph Kiner, who were not good defensive players and probably would have been DHs if they were playing today. Would you deny them admittance to the Hall of Fame? I don't think so.

Another category that needs to be examined is relief pitchers, who for years were denied entry into the Hall of Fame. But now Hoyt Wilhelm, Rollie Fingers, Dennis Eckersley, and Bruce Sutter are in, and soon to follow will be Goose Gossage and maybe Lee Smith. Then there's Trevor Hoffman, the all-time saves leader, and Mariano Rivera, with the lowest earned-run average in postseason history, both Hall of Famers-in-waiting.

Among active pitchers, you have to say it's a lock for 300-game winners Roger Clemens (many say he's the greatest pitcher in baseball history), Greg Maddux, and Tom Glavine. Randy Johnson, who's close to 300 wins, and Pedro Martinez, with 3,000 strikeouts and three Cy Young Awards, are also certain inductees.

Ken Griffey Jr. is a no-brainer. I think Craig Biggio should be elected. Also Pudge Rodriguez and Mike Piazza and, when their time comes, Alex Rodriguez, Derek Jeter, Vladimir Guerrero, and Albert Pujols.

Chipper Jones has to be strongly considered, and so does Omar Vizquel, a shortstop who has been compared with Luis Aparicio and Ozzie Smith, both in the Hall of

Fame. Also Jeff Kent, who has better offensive numbers than any other second baseman except Rogers Hornsby. And Ichiro Suzuki is certain to be the first player from Japan to be elected to the Hall of Fame when he becomes eligible.

I don't see how Ichiro can miss, especially with his new five-year contract extension that will give him the 10 years of major league service required for Hall of Fame eligibility. He's a tremendous all-around player and a great hitter. He holds the major league record for hits in a season with 262 in 2004 and a major league career batting average of .333. In Japan, he racked up 1,278 hits in nine seasons, and then he came to the United States and had more than 200 hits and a plus-.300 batting average in each of his first seven seasons. He's on pace to compile more than 4,000 hits in the United States and Japan combined.

To go with his magic bat, Ichiro is an outstanding defensive outfielder with a great arm, and he's an exceptional runner who has averaged almost 40 steals per year for his first seven seasons. He's more of a singles hitter than a power hitter, but he can hit home runs if he wants to, as indicated by his 13 dingers in 2003 and 15 in 2005. In 2007 he became the first player ever to hit an inside-the-park home run in the All-Star Game.

And then there are players like Todd Helton, Ryan Howard, Miguel Cabrera, Carl Crawford, Chase Utley, and others who have started off their careers as potential Hall of Famers. We'll just have to wait a few years to see if they can keep it up before we pass judgment on their Hall of Fame credentials.

The bottom line is there are a lot of modern-day players who will be elected to the Hall of Fame in the future. It's going to be exciting to be a part of the fraternity and to see those guys being inducted, just as it was for me in 2007 to see Cal Ripken Jr. and Tony Gwynn inducted. Those are two players you have to admire and respect because not only were they great players and great ambassadors for the game, but they're both great people as well.

It's going to be exciting to be a part of the fraternity and to see those guys being inducted, just as it was for me in 2007 to see Cal Ripken Jr. and Tony Gwynn inducted.

To me, that's what the Hall of Fame is all about.

Afterword

SHORTLY BEFORE THIS BOOK WENT TO PRESS, I LANDED a job as a manager.

I had contacted just about every major league team to see if there were any openings as a major league coach or a minor league manager or coach, but there was nothing doing. It was a humbling experience to say the least to discover that there was no room in organized baseball for a 19-year veteran who was willing to accept the hard work, the difficult travel, and the 14 hour days that are required in the minor leagues.

I had pretty much given up hope when I received an offer to manage the Orange County Flyers in the independent Golden Baseball League, a team based in my birthplace, Fullerton, California.

It's not the major leagues. It's not even a minor league team with a major league affiliation, but it's baseball and that's the main thing.

I'm excited about this new opportunity for several reasons, not the least of which is being back in uniform and afforded a chance to work toward my ultimate goal, to be a major league manager.

This new position is ideal because I will be going "home" and it will give me a chance to spend time with my brother, Gordon, who lives in nearby Santa Ana; my son, D.J., the aspiring actor who lives about an hour away in Venice; my in-laws; and one of my dearest friends, Doug Jones, who live in Fullerton.

Thinking about managing a team in my home town, where I grew up, went to grade school and high school, brings back a flood of memories of my early days in California, all the way back to Little League, Pony League, and American Legion ball. I can't help but think of people like Bob Robbins who had the best pick-off move to third base in American Legion ball when I was the batboy for my brother Gordy's team.

The Golden Baseball League is a six-team league with teams in Fullerton, Chico, and Long Beach, California; and Reno, Nevada; St. George, Utah; and Yuma, Arizona. We play a 76-game schedule that begins the first week of June and ends the final week of August.

Our 44 home games will be played at Cal State–Fullerton College and there are several Sundays with no games scheduled, so there will be ample opportunity for me to spend time with my family and friends. Furthermore, the Flyers have generously offered to fly Sandy out several times during the season.

If we're fortunate enough to make the playoffs that will add another week to the season, so my total commitment will be more than 15 weeks. My goal is to bring a Golden

Baseball League championship to my hometown and I will devote all my energy to make that happen.

I am a firm believer that things happen for a reason and my faith tells me that this is where God wants me to be.

As I reflect upon my life at the age of 54, I can say I have truly been blessed in so many ways: blessed with a great family, blessed with a great career. I have realized all the aspirations and dreams I had since I was a kid.

Now, a new door has opened for me and with it, two things can be accomplished. I will get to spend some time with family and friends and I will get back into the game.

However, I also have come to the realization that you don't always get what you wish for, and I'm okay with that. I have so much to look forward to. Yes, my desire still is to manage in the major leagues, but if it doesn't happen, I'll move on. I'll always want to be productive, and I'll always want to do something because that has been a part of my life: to have a purpose and to accomplish something in the course of the day.

I have always been motivated. All along I have wanted to try to be the best at whatever I do. I never wanted to accept second best. My whole life I have been performance-oriented. It was pounded into me from day one. I got my greatest praise from my dad when I was successful on the playing field.

I was my happiest when I was playing. I couldn't wait to get to the ballpark every day, and I loved every minute of it. I am privileged that God gave me the talent to play Major League Baseball, an opportunity that comes to so very few. I love this game. I always will. I can't describe how exhilarating it is to play in front of large crowds as I had the pleasure of doing for five years in New York, when we averaged more than 40,000 fans per game; when you have done something that elicits cheers and applause from a big crowd, nothing can replace that, and I miss it.

The great thing about baseball is that you can go 0-for-4 and still help your team win by doing the job defensively: a play at the plate, a great catch, a great throw. Or you can get four hits and be disappointed because you lost the game, and yet still have some gratification because much of your recognition is based on what you do individually.

My greatest feeling as a player was after a game, after talking to the press, meeting with the trainers to get ice on the bumps and bruises, then walking out of the clubhouse and there was my family. Nothing could replace that.

I never was satisfied until I walked onto the field before a game, looked up into the stands, and saw my wife and kids sitting there. I would tug at my ear, or point, or nod my head: some sign of acknowledgment. That's an experience most men don't have. How many men are privileged to have their family observe them in their workplace?

If I had a bad game, they were there to pick me up. I took failure hard as a player. I was always hard on myself. I expected perfection. But I tried never to let my failure affect my family, and they would be waiting for me after the game with open arms to ease my anguish with a smile, a kind word, a hug. Failure made me look forward to the next game. If I had a bad game, I couldn't wait for the next day, when I could brush off the failure and try to do better.

There's no question that the highlight, the culmination, and the overall reward of my career was being elected to the Hall of Fame. That was the pinnacle of my life as a ballplayer, especially being able to share it with my family and so many of my close friends, all the way back to Bob Robbins, who had the best pickoff move to third base in American Legion ball when I was the batboy for my brother Gordy's team.

Along with being elected to the Hall of Fame, the other great reward of my baseball career was playing on the team, the New York Mets, that won the World Series in 1986. It's what every professional baseball player aspires to, and I am fortunate to have had the experience. It can never be taken away from me. I'm not one for jewelry, but I wear my World Series ring with pride.

Did I pay a price? Of course I did. I've had to go through a great deal after my playing career, with the many surgeries I had. I've had my right knee replaced, and eventually I'm going to have my left knee done. But as I said before, baseball has given me my identity. Without baseball I would be just another guy, not Gary Carter, former major league player and Hall of Famer.

Baseball also has given me the opportunity to provide for my family, and I wouldn't trade my baseball career for anything.

I remember the good times, and I am fortunate to be able to reflect on those good times when I'm sitting in my office at home. I can look at the walls and see the picture of me jumping into the arms of Jesse Orosco after the final out of the 1986 World Series, or the picture of me with Mickey Mantle, my boyhood idol, or of my mom and me at the "Punt, Pass and Kick" competition when I was just a little guy. I feel like I am in a different world when I'm sitting in my office at home looking around and thinking of all the great things that have happened in my life. I truly have been a blessed man.

I have been out of the game as a player for more than 16 years, and the toughest thing for any athlete—and I have talked to many former athletes about this—is that you miss what you have done for so many years. When you have reached a certain height in your career and suddenly it's over, you miss what you once had: the competition, the fellowship with teammates, and the cheers of the crowd.

I want to stay in baseball. I want to give back to the game because I believe I have so much to give. I would like the opportunity to one day be a manager on the major league level.

None of us knows what the future is going to bring. I don't know what's in my future. But I have faith. I don't know what the future holds, but I do know who holds the future. I truly believe God has a plan for me.

As it says in Jeremiah 29:12, "'For I know the plans I have for you,' declares the Lord, 'plans to prosper you and not to harm you, plans to give you hope and a future.'"

God blessed me with a wonderful life. I'm grateful for the 54 years I've lived to this point. Baseball enables you to remain a kid no matter what your age. I'll always love the game of baseball, and I'll always be a "Kid."

Appendix

ON JULY 27, 2003, GARY CARTER, ALONG WITH SPORTS-writer Hal McCoy of the Dayton *Daily News,* broadcaster Bob Uecker, and Eddie Murray, was formally inducted into the Baseball Hall of Fame. After Hall of Fame board of directors chairman Jane Forbes Clark introduced a short video of Carter's career and baseball commissioner Bud Selig read the words on Carter's Hall of Fame plaque, Gary addressed the multitude. His speech follows:

> *Wow!*
> *Are you having fun?*
> *Thank you, Jane. And thank you, Bud.*
> *You know that feeling as a kid when you go into a candy store for the first time? All you can do is smile and just stand in awe. Well, this "Kid" is in the candy store today. Cooperstown, where all dreams come true. Can you feel it? It is so sweet.*
> *There are so many people to thank today that have influenced my life and my career. I've been*

told by the other Hall of Famers that I have a time limit. Twenty minutes. Those of you that know me, [know] this is going to be difficult. All right. I have a tendency to elaborate at times, so I am going to try to do my best. Just bear with me. I would be remiss if I did not say a few words in French. So here goes.

Bonjour Madames et Monsieurs, M. President, et les invites distingues. C'est avec grand plaisir et grand honneur d'etre ici aujourd'hui. J'aimerais remercier tous le participants, les Expos, Mets, Giants et Dodgers. Mes amis, merci boucoup.

I would like to thank all the sportswriters, obviously, for this tremendous honor. I would also like to congratulate Hal McCoy for his great journalism through the years. All the pleasant times coming into the clubhouse. And Bob Uecker, for all the fantastic years of broadcasting. Now, Ueck, you'll never be in the cheap seats again, pal, because you'll always be in the front row.

I am so humbled to stand before you all and be in the presence of all these great Hall of Famers. This has been a terrific weekend, and I would like to thank all the people involved with the Hall of Fame. From Dale Petroskey to Jane Clark to Jeff Idelson to Kim Bennett and, of course, all of the other staff members.

I had a dream as a young boy, like all of these Hall of Famers up here, to be a professional athlete. I was blessed with a gift, and I thank the Lord above for the wonderful, wonderful opportunity to have played this great game of baseball.

I played all the sports as a young boy, but it was always baseball that I loved the most. I collected baseball cards as a hobby and one day dreamed of what it would be like to have my picture on one of those cards. I grew up in Southern California, a Dodgers fan, and my idol was the Mick, Mickey Mantle. I know you're here with us today, Mick, so thank you for instilling in me the love of the game. You see, I always have been a fan of the game first and a ballplayer second. Maybe that's why I had the love and passion for this great game so much.

My dream became a reality in 1972, when the Montreal Expos drafted me in the third round. In high school, my main sport was football as an All-American quarterback. Most of my scholarship offers from colleges were for football, not baseball. So I had to think and pray hard and long to help make my decision. My decision was altered after a serious knee injury, which resulted in sitting out my entire senior football season, but I was looking so forward to playing my passion, baseball.

It is funny because my primary positions in high school were as a pitcher and an infielder. I only caught five or six games my senior year of high school. But during those five or six games a scout by the name of Bob Zuk, who is here with us today, believed I could become a big-league catcher some day. He held true to his word, and on the night of the draft, at 18 years of age, I signed a contract with the Expos and started making plans to head off to Jamestown, New York. Bob, thanks for believing in me.

So off I went to New York for a two-week try-out camp to determine where I was going to play that year. And it was there that Bill McKenzie, my first catching coach, taught me all the fundamentals and techniques about catching. He was the one who taught me how to catch. Thanks, Bill, for your motivation and discipline. I don't know if you're here today, but I just want to thank you for everything that you did for me.

And it was there in Jamestown, New York, where the journey began. I would like to thank all the coaches and managers I played for. From my very first manager, Pat Daugherty, to my very last manager, Felipe Alou, in Montreal. However, there is one manager who has left such an impact on my life and in my career and that was Karl Kuehl, who is with us today. He managed me when I was in the Instructional League, AA, and AAA, and I know he believed in me more than anyone else. I remember he would throw tennis balls to me, worked on my hitting, and to get out of the way of pitches. And he would even charge me 25¢ for every ball that I would drop when I was catching in a game.

This, of course, helped me concentrate better and helped me focus. And truly, I dropped a lot of balls when I was playing in the minor leagues, so this really did help. Although, at the end of the year, Karl said, "Aw, you don't owe me anything." Karl, thanks for working so hard with me and for helping me be a better ballplayer.

I would like to thank all of my teammates, some of them that are in the audience today. Thank you for inspiring me, making the game more fun and enjoyable. A lot of great memories that I will never forget.

After two and a half years in the minor leagues being groomed as a catcher, I began my rookie season in the major leagues in 1975. The Expos started me in the outfield. Well, that was when I could run pretty good and had some pretty decent knees. But after having a pretty good first half, I was invited to the All-Star Game in Milwaukee. Well, there it was Johnny Bench who befriended me and kind of took me under his wing. By then Johnny had established himself as one of, if not the best, defensive catchers there ever was. Maybe, just maybe, he saw a little of him in me.

We had a picture taken together, and later I asked him if he would sign it for me. And he wrote on it, he said, "Kid, in a few years, it's all yours." Well, that inspired me to carry the torch for catchers, because it made me want to work as hard as possible and try to make every All-Star Game, and be the best at my position. Thanks, J.B., I appreciate it very much.

I was sitting there talking to Eddie [Murray] and he says, "You're the one who chose those tools of ignorance," but, really, I always considered them being the tools of excellence. And there is something special, I truly feel, about being a catcher that only another catcher can understand. So, Yogi, Pudge, J.B., you know what I'm talking about. It is an honor to enjoy being a part of this great fraternity.

Well, after two and a half years of playing mostly in the outfield, I finally got a chance to play every day behind the plate in 1977. Dick Williams was instrumental in making that happen. From that point on, the rest was history. You see, going to a baseball game, just like you guys are here today, and sitting in the stands is like going to that happy place where you can leave your worries behind.

One of my favorite lines comes from a movie, Field of Dreams, and it goes something like this:

> This game, this great game, is as innocent as children longing for the past. The feeling you get when you go to a ballgame, walking through the aisles to your seats, sitting in your shirtsleeves on a perfect afternoon. You find your reserve seat somewhere along the baselines, and

acting as if you were a kid again. It's almost as though you dipped yourself in magical waters that the memories will be so thick you have to brush them away from your face. Yes, the one constant through all the years has been baseball. America has rolled by like an army of steamrollers. It has been erased like a blackboard, built and erased again, but baseball has marked the time. America's pastime.

Baseball has allowed me to meet so many special people along the way. One here today that I am so honored to have in our presence is former President George Bush Sr. He has been such a great friend through the years, and I appreciate very much the effort of you coming to today's ceremony with your grandson, Robert, and I just want to thank you from the bottom of my heart, Mr. President. God bless you.

A few more people who kept me on track, especially on the business side of baseball, were Dick Moss and Matt Merola. They couldn't be here today, but thank you guys for helping me with all the contracts and endorsements through the years.

I'd also like to especially thank one particular good friend, and that's Jerry Petrie, who not only was instrumental and was such a great guy and became such a good friend in Montreal, but he also was my agent. He represented me in all aspects as an agent, and I appreciated the guidance and direction that he gave me. He encouraged me to be accommodating to the press, the fans, and made sure I always looked my best. Pete, thanks for everything.

I also want to extend a very special thank you to my good friend, Mead Chasky. I have known this man for a long time, when he was a huge fan and would hang around the team bus and would get autographs from all the players. I tell you what, he's now my manager and he's been the best man for this job to handle so many things for me. You're awesome, Mead, and I can't thank you enough. What a godsend you have been.

The greatest thrill of my career certainly was that amazing '86 World Series. Nothing will ever top that and the memories will last forever. All of you that were there, everybody, will remember the dramatic Game 6 and certainly the way we came back in that Series. So all of you Mets fans, God bless you, '86.

I will be forever grateful to the Expos for beginning my career and winding up my career in 1992. The Lord gave me a storybook ending of my career in front of over 40,000 fans. My last at-bat was a game-winning double, and after hobbling to second base I left the game to a standing ovation. There is nothing like the roar of the crowd.

Now I'd like to take this moment to say what an honor it is to share this day with you, Eddie. Even though we only shared one year together with the Dodgers, I always respected your desire and your professionalism. A lot of people don't know Eddie Murray the way I do, and it was in spring training in 1991, after one of the games, Eddie headed back to the clubhouse with a bat that he had broken in the game. In the midst of a large crowd, Eddie handed that broken bat to a smiling little boy. That boy happened to be my son, D.J. He was only six years old at the time, and he ran in to the clubhouse to show me what he had just gotten. I was kind of shocked because, Eddie, you don't share a lot of things with a lot of people, you know. But anyway, I walked over to him and asked him if he would kindly sign it, and, after a brief hesitation, he did and, well, today D.J. considers that bat one of his most prized possessions. And that, right there, was the start of a Carter-Murray connection. Who would have believed that we'd be standing here today, on July 27, 2003, being inducted with all these great players?

Okay, this is where it might get a little tough. I want to take this time to thank the most important people in my life. Above all, I want to thank my Lord and savior, Jesus Christ. A great verse that spoke to me while writing my speech and kind of explains what it is all about, it comes in Psalms 18: "I love you, Lord, you are my strength. The Lord is my rock, my fortress, and my savior. And my God is my rock in whom I find protection. He is my shield, the strength of my salvation, and my stronghold. I will call on the Lord who is worthy of praise. I praise the Lord, my God, my best friend, for giving me the ability, the desire, the love, and the guidance that brought me here today. Without you, I would be nothing."

I thank the Lord for giving me such wonderful parents. My parents can't be here today in person, and I know they are smiling down from heaven today, because they have the best seats in the house. I have said to a lot of people that my father's on my right shoulder today and my mom's on my left. I love my parents very, very much. I only had my mother until I was just 12 years of age, but I always felt her presence throughout my career.

My father, Jim, who inherited the responsibility of both parents, didn't have a mean bone in his body and always had a smile for everyone. He was always there for me. He coached me in Little League, Pony League, and American Legion and also supported me in any other sport I played, constantly encouraging me. His favorite time of year was spring training, when he'd come visit the family and watch a few games. He would go early with me to the ballpark and would *stay until the end. He just couldn't get enough baseball. I'll never forget the time when we were playing cards in the clubhouse and the manager called a team meeting. That meant everyone out of the clubhouse, except the team. Well, my dad's response was, "Do I have to? I have a pretty good hand." Well, if you know my pop, that's the way he was. And Mom, Pop, you're missed, but you'll never be forgotten. I know how happy and proud you guys are today.*

I am also very blessed to have my other parents, my in-laws, Mom and Dad, my brother-in-law, Jim, who are with me today. They have known me since I was 16 years old and have watched me grow up. Thanks for all your love and support throughout the years and always opening up your home in California for after-game celebrations.

Well, as for my big brother, Gordon, who is four years older than me, I thank you for being such an amazing role model for me growing up. It meant so much to me that you would allow me to always play ball with you and your friends, even if I did bug you all the time. You have been the one who has influenced me to always strive to do my best. I always tried to be your shadow and looked up to you in so many ways. I realize now how much you did for me while growing up. I am so thankful for the relationship we have. I love you, big brother.

Well, to my immediate family, there is so much to say and not enough time to say it. So, the one thing I remember the most is how much the kids and Sandy would be at all the games. You know, I never felt comfortable or relaxed until I saw their happy faces sitting in the stands behind home plate. What a blessing I truly have had for my wife and my kids to be right there with me through it all. After each game, I would always be the last player to leave the clubhouse. It still amazes me to look back and think about the many hours my family waited for me without complaining. It was funny, because if I had a good game or if the team won, the kids knew the car ride home would be a heck of a lot more fun. To my three precious children, I love you all very, very much, and I am so proud of each and every one of you and for all that you have done. I am so thankful that each of you have chosen to walk with the Lord.

Christy, you remember the most about my career, and have always prayed that I would do well in games. You were my number-one cheer-leader. What a help you were to Mom and a great role model to Kimmy and D.J. You have become a beautiful woman and an excellent teacher. To my new son-in-law, Matt Kearce, who I feel is like a second son already, thanks for taking care of my kiddo.

To my little catcher, Kimmy, who would sometimes only last a couple of innings before she would head off to the wives' room and start up her own games. She played softball with the same kind of passion and desire that I did. I got the chance to coach her, and I was amazed to see how much she reminded me of myself on the field. I certainly wouldn't want to try to slide into her, either, because, I tell you, she could some kind of block the plate. And she also left her mark at Florida State University. She enjoys teaching kids in the classroom and on the field, and she has truly turned out to be a beautiful woman, inside and out.

To my son, D.J. What a phenomenal man you have become. No father could ever be more proud of his son than I am of you. You light up on stage, and you light up any room you enter. You are the most encouraging person and positive person I know. D.J., you inspire me, bud, to be a better man.

As for my wife and high school sweetheart, and now wife of over 28 years, I fell in love with you, honey, when I was 16, and my love for you has remained constant through the years. I thank you always for your encouraging words and all the letters you wrote to me while in the minor leagues. And for taking care of the family, and for always being by my side. You have truly shown your love to me and have always been the wind beneath my wings. For that I will be forever grateful. I share this day with you, honey, more than anyone else here. I love you more than you'll ever know.

And in closing, [to those] I have mentioned and for so many that I have not been able to mention, thank you from the bottom of my heart. It is nice to know that even though my body feels like an old man now, I will always be a kid at heart. I love this great game. I'm so honored to be in Cooperstown as a Hall of Famer. I love you all. God bless you. Thank you very much.

Reprinted by permission of the National Baseball Hall of Fame.